D0502495

"*The Heart-Led Leader* will not only help you become the person you want to be—it will help you become the person that you know you should be. Follow Tommy's lessons and it will change your life as well as the lives of those you serve and lead."

—Marshall Goldsmith, *New York Times* bestselling author of *Triggers, MOJO,* and *What Got You Here Won't Get You There*

"A powerful read that can profoundly change the way you approach leading any team. The inspiring stories in *The Heart-Led Leader* give clear examples of how others have transformed their companies by leading with the heart. A must-read for everyone in my organization."

—John Ruble, global vice president of sales operations and talent development, Marriott Vacations Worldwide

"*The Heart-Led Leader* brilliantly captures the essence of building extraordinary teams: the matrix of caring and unselfish, trust-your-life relationships. Flawless performance matters in human spaceflight, but at the end of the day heart-guided leadership is what really drives mission success."

—Colonel Rick Searfoss, astronaut, Space Shuttle commander, and author of *Liftoff*

"This book holds the keys to driving bottom-line results through what Tommy Spaulding calls Heart-Led Leadership. These stories will challenge you to balance your bright mind with an engaged heart—a leadership approach that will help you love those you lead."

—Cheryl Bachelder, CEO of Popeyes Louisiana Kitchen and author of *Dare to Serve*

"Tommy Spaulding teaches us in his new book, *The Heart-Led Leader,* what I have always believed and practiced, which is, you must go through the heart to reach the brain. Leaders who practice this approach will achieve far greater results and leave a legacy of excellence in all parts of their life."

—Lee Cockerell, former executive vice president of Walt Disney World Resort and author of *Creating Magic*

"There are few differentiators left in business. In *The Heart-Led Leader* Tommy Spaulding explores how leaders who lead with heart create workplaces that are not only inspiring, but that deliver superior results. If you want to become a better leader you need to read this book!"

—Chester Elton, *New York Times* bestselling author of *The Carrot Principle, All In,* and *What Motivates Me*

"Inspiring and persuasive. Tommy gives real-life examples on how leaders have changed their lives, their businesses, and their communities, by living their principles of leading through the 'heart.'"

—Hoyt Jones, president of Jersey Mike's Franchise Systems

"The real-life examples of 'Heart-Led Leadership' are not only inspiring but could be a game changer in our lives and in our organizations if put into practice. Tommy's philosophy of connecting with and caring for others is the key to being a powerful leader."

—Scott Sibella, president and COO of MGM Grand

"*The Heart-Led Leader* wonderfully proves that love and leadership not only are deeply interconnected, but are the seeds for extraordinary results."

—Dylan Taylor, global COO of Colliers International

"I first met Tommy through the organizational transformation work he specializes in. As the CEO of a company that doubles every few years, my team lives his message. Our work is extremely dangerous: I've led teams to the summits of Mount Everest, K2, and more than a hundred other peaks on five continents. You have to know who you are, since the consequences of being less than the very best 'you' can be fatal."

—Chris Warner, CEO of Earth Treks and
author of *High Altitude Leadership*

"Tommy's real-life and compelling stories of heart-led leadership illuminate the very core of your soul. This 18-inch 'love wins' credo inspires you to place loving and serving others center stage. A must-read for anyone who is held accountable for bottom-line results."

—Jayne Hladio, senior vice president and
regional executive of U.S. Bank

"We live in a business environment that is extraordinarily complicated and in constant flux. Although critical thinking and astute strategy are crucial for success, both are useless without connecting back to the source for all great ideas: the heart. Tommy Spaulding reminds us of this truth and provides specific ways that we can journey those 18 critical inches from our heads to our hearts."

—John O'Leary, founder of Rising Above and author of *On Fire*

"*The Heart-Led Leader* is in the top 2 leadership books of the last decade. I believe it will launch a movement that will transform leadership philosophy forever."

—Rick Barrera, bestselling author of *Overpromise and Overdeliver*

"Eighteen short—but important—inches. In his heartfelt book, Tommy Spaulding compassionately leads us on a journey from the head to the heart. Through eighteen different stories with themes ranging from character to humility to vulnerability to result-driven purpose, *The Heart-Led Leader* provides a roadmap to explore the true meaning of oneself in order to help lead with EQ rather than IQ."

—John Hayes, president and CEO of Ball Corporation

"Tommy puts into words what I've always lived and believed—the best and most fulfilling leadership is heart-led servant leadership. Take Tommy's 18-inch journey from your head to your heart and you will not only increase your bottom line, but change the lives of those you lead. This is required reading for my entire leadership team."

—Buddy Brown, president of Independent Hardee's Franchise Association

"Whether you are an accomplished leader or just getting started, Tommy Spaulding's *The Heart-Led Leader* will compel you to rethink your relationships, your leadership philosophy, and what you really want out of life. Through the lens of his own relationships and experiences, Tommy offers powerful insights and a practical tool kit you can start working with right away to achieve breakthrough results."

—John Swieringa, SVP and CIO of Dish Network LLC

"Being a heart-led leader is easy for Tommy Spaulding because these traits come so naturally to him. This is not a leadership style that he turns off and on. . . . It is how he lives his life. But now he's written a manual to teach us all his secret sauce. A life-, business-, and career-changing read!"

—John Ikard, chairman of American Bankers Association

"In a world consumed by a relentless climb to the top, Tommy Spaulding has lived by example showing me and everyone who knows him that there is a more fulfilling way to live and lead—one that leaves a lasting legacy behind you. This book is a must-read and a reminder of what true leadership looks like."

—Matthew West, ASCAP Christian Music Songwriter/ Artist of the Year winner and four-time Grammy nominee

"Every educator in America must read Tommy Spaulding's new book, *The Heart-Led Leader*. When you read it, do so with the intent to be changed! Through Tommy's riveting stories, your heart will grow as you go on an 18-inch journey transforming you to a leader who leads with your heart. Be ready to embrace leadership in a new and life-changing way."

—Dr. Jim Wipke, superintendent of Fox School District, Missouri

"*The Heart-Led Leader* is an important book because it not only speaks about servant leadership and how it impacts people, but also is one of the first of its kind to connect this leadership philosophy to bottom-line results. And with his tear-jerking storytelling, Tommy Spaulding writes the book in a way that makes it hard to put down."

—Walt Rakowich, former CEO and president of Prologis

"Spot on! Tommy Spaulding artfully weaves the value of solid business practices with his trademark storytelling and insights how heart-led leadership impacts the lives we lead and clients we serve. A powerful read for anybody in sales or leadership positions who are responsible for bottom-line performance."

—Chris Mygatt, president of Coldwell Banker
Residential Brokerage–Colorado

"The leader must first and foremost: Love. As Tommy Spaulding explains in this wonderful book, the journey starts in the heart. Read this book to take your leadership impact to the next level."

—Tim Sanders, author of *Love Is the Killer App*

"As a fervent believer in relationship-driven leadership, I strongly recommend that all leaders (or those who wish to become leaders) read this book. Tommy Spaulding identifies, explains, and exemplifies what is missing from most leaders' arsenals—the power of heart-driven leadership."

—Stuart Holland, VP–Retail Sales of Pacific Life Insurance

"Tommy Spaulding is the real deal. Since the first time I met him, I've suspected he has an oversized heart, due to his uncanny ability to pump a steady stream of love to everyone he meets, either through his speaking engagements, his writings, or his personal relationships. In *The Heart-Led Leader*, Tommy reminds us that we already possess the capability for unbridled success—all we need is love."

—Eric Blehm, *New York Times* bestselling author of *Fearless* and *Legend*

"The first leadership book I could NOT put down. The pages flow in this must-read masterpiece by Tommy Spaulding. *The Heart-Led Leader* is truly inspirational and full of essential leadership lessons for new and experienced leaders alike."

—Chris Howard, president of hospital operations,
SSM Health Care

ALSO BY TOMMY SPAULDING

It's Not Just Who You Know:
Transform Your Life (and Your Organization)
by Turning Colleagues and Contacts
into Lasting, Genuine Relationships

THE
HEART-LED
LEADER

How Living and
Leading from the Heart
Will Change Your
Organization and Your Life

TOMMY SPAULDING

CROWN
BUSINESS
NEW YORK

Published in the United States by Crown Business, an imprint of the Crown
Publishing Group, a division of Penguin Random House LLC, New York.
www.crownpublishing.com

CROWN BUSINESS is a trademark and CROWN and the Rising Sun colophon are
registered trademarks of Penguin Random House LLC.

Crown Business books are available at special discounts for bulk purchases for
sales promotions or corporate use. Special editions, including personalized covers,
excerpts of existing books, or books with corporate logos, can be created in large
quantities for special needs. For more information, contact Premium Sales at
(212) 572-2232 or e-mail specialmarkets@penguinrandomhouse.com.

Library of Congress Cataloging-in-Publication Data
Spaulding, Tommy. The Heart-Led Leader : how living and leading from the heart
will change your organization and your life / Thomas Spaulding.
Includes index. 1. Leadership. I. Title.
HD57.7.S69426   2015
658.4'092—dc23   2015007697

ISBN 978-0-553-41903-0
eBook ISBN 978-0-553-41904-7

Printed in the United States of America

Book design by Helene Berinksy

10 9 8 7 6 5 4 3 2 1

First Edition

Dedicated to my wife, Jill,
my daughter, Caroline,
and my mother, Diane Marino—
the most important women in my life.

CONTENTS

PART THREE

LEAVING A *HEART*PRINT ON THE WORLD

Introduction:
Love-Driven Results

—————

THE JOURNEY TO HEART-LED LEADERSHIP COVERS ONLY 18 INCHES, but it lasts a lifetime.

That's where I want to take you with this book—on an 18-inch journey, the distance from your head to your heart.

It starts with these important questions: Who are you? Who do you want to become? What do you want to be known for as a person and as a leader? And what is your leadership philosophy?

If you don't have a leadership philosophy, that's OK. Most leaders don't have a specific philosophy, at least not one they can name. I hope to change that. I hope you'll choose to become a heart-led leader, or what I call a Who Leader. I want this for you because it will change your life, your organization, and the lives of everyone you touch. And if you do it right, it will also change the lives of everyone they touch. I will prove to you in this book the game-changing impact of heart-led leadership. If you want to have that kind of impact in the world, you have found your leadership philosophy.

But only if you're willing to let it change your heart.

The heart, of course, is nothing more than a wonderful metaphor. For centuries, the muscle that pumps blood throughout our bodies has also been known as the keeper of our emotions. We use the heart to describe how we feel, how the world around us moves us, and how people and experiences change the very essence of who we are at the deepest, most intimate levels.

Leading from the heart means leading with love. If the word *love* scares you, then use *passion, commitment, compassion, servant leadership, purpose-driven, mission-driven,* or your choice of any similar word or phrase, because at the core these are all forms of love. In this context, love is simply an unselfish and genuine concern for the good of others. So when we lead from the heart—when we lead with love—we care deeply about serving others, about selflessness, about doing the right thing even when it's difficult, about developing empathy and demonstrating generosity, about all those ideals that may seem "soft" but, in fact, allow us to live and lead more powerfully.

Defining your leadership philosophy is one of the most important steps you can take as a leader. Your philosophy filters every thought and action you take as a leader. Every decision you make and every conversation you have with your team are reflections of who you are. And when you take the 18-inch journey to heart-led leadership—and it's definitely a journey—you will continually define and refine who you are.

IN 2010 I WROTE *It's Not Just Who You Know,* a best-selling book about the power of building lasting, genuine relationships in our lives and in our workplaces. The final chapter ends with these words: "It's not just who you know—it's who you are."

I've been amazed and humbled by the reaction to that book, and I believe more strongly than ever in its message. But I've also come to realize that the impact of those final four words—"it's who you are"—goes far beyond relationships or the ways in which you connect with people. Who you are goes to the very core of how you live, how you serve, and how you lead.

My unlikely journey began as a dyslexic kid in a small village in upstate New York, and it has taken me all over the planet and put me in a position to listen to and learn from some of the best leaders in some of the world's top-performing organizations. I've met thousands of leaders in my career, and I make it a point to learn as much as I can from every one of them. In all of my conversations, one thing has become abundantly clear: leaders and organizations that lead with their hearts are more successful and drive better results than those that don't.

Love and results are not opposites. They are two sides of the same coin. It is not love *or* results. It is *love-driven results.*

If you love what you do, if you love the people you do it with, if you love your culture, if you love your mission, if you love your team, if you love your investors, if you love your clients, if you love your customers—you will gain better results. Period.

There are many ways to make money, build businesses, and achieve goals that don't involve leading from the heart. If you think that business is purely about earning a living, making money, and driving profits, then I believe you're missing the real meaning of life and, more important, limiting your impact on the world.

Heart-led leadership transcends numbers and spreadsheets. It is more sustainable and more rewarding. It also inspires, encourages, and influences the world for the better. And that leads to even greater results, because it creates passionate teams—teams that believe in the mission, teams that provide discretionary effort (effort beyond what's required of them), teams that model heart-led leadership and pass it on to others. It provides everything any business leader would want—higher sales, better margins, greater employee engagement with less turnover, stronger teams, greater efficiencies, more innovation, and consistent growth. You name the positive business outcome and I believe you will find heart-led leadership is at its core.

Hear me loud and clear. I do not advocate heart-led

leadership because of some touchy-feely, utopian, kum-baya belief. I advocate it because it is the fastest, most powerful way to drive cold, hard, pragmatic bottom-line results and impact for your organization, and I intend to prove this to you in stories throughout this book.

When this type of love—this heart-led leadership—is modeled at all levels of an organization, then the positive results multiply into a remarkable and sustainable force. I've seen the positive results of heart-led leadership in some of the most unexpected places.

I've seen how a Who Leader, Tee Green, built a medi-cal software company that was so valued for its heart-led leadership that when it was purchased for $644 million and merged with a company six times its size, the new company retained the Greenway Health name and kept Green as the CEO.

I've seen how a Who Leader, Cheryl Bachelder, took over a restaurant chain struggling with a long history of declining sales and profits and used heart-led leadership to help grow its stock price by 450 percent over six years.

I've seen how a Who Leader, Frank DeAngelis, took a high school where thirteen students and teachers lost their lives in a mass shooting and used heart-led leader-ship to overcome that tragedy and transform the school's culture into one of love, hope, and promise.

I've seen how a Who Leader, Chris Warner, used heart-led leadership lessons to lead a team of mountain climbers up K2, where nearly 25 percent of summit attempts end in death, and to become one of only nine Americans to ever stand on the peaks of the world's two highest mountains, Everest and K2.

I've seen how a Who Leader, Walt Rakowich, took an S&P global real estate corporation that was on the brink of bankruptcy (its stock price had dropped 95 percent and its market capitalization had dropped from $20 billion to less than $1 billion) and restored it to profitability by practicing heart-led leadership.

I've seen how a Who Leader, Warden Burl Cain, took the largest, most dangerous maximum-security prison in America and changed it, using heart-led leadership, into a place so safe that in-prison assaults dropped 70 percent in 15 years and inmates serving life sentences without parole now sell popcorn and cotton candy to kids at the prison's annual rodeo.

I'll share those stories and many more in the pages of this book, because they can help you—as they helped me—develop deeper insights into what it means to live, love, and lead as a heart-led leader.

The Heart-Led Leader is the product of the life lessons formed from decades of experiences that have changed me for the better. Some of these lessons are a result of my personal experiences and my successes and failures in life; others were shared with me by the incredible individuals who have crossed my path—CEOs, entrepreneurs, school principals, sales executives, coaches, Olympians, rock stars, astronauts, mountain climbers, and friends.

You might think that this type of leadership philosophy—this ability to lead from the heart—is reserved for certain personality types or for leaders who have risen to the top of their organizations. But I've discovered that heart-led leadership exists at all levels of organizations and in companies of all types and sizes. Heart-led leaders are in nonprofits, start-ups, schools, faith-based organizations, small businesses, and Fortune 500 companies. They work in cubicles and in corner offices.

What if you embrace heart-led leadership as your leadership philosophy?

I know for certain that your life will change—for the better. The lives of your employees, co-workers, clients, customers, friends, and family will change—for the better. The lives of people in your communities will change—for the better. And your organizations will change—for the better.

I know this because I've seen it. I know this because I've lived it.

And you can live it, too, if you decide to take this 18-inch journey with me.

PART ONE

BECOMING A
HEART-LED LEADER

Who You Are Matters

ONE OF THE PEOPLE WHO TAUGHT ME THE MOST ABOUT BEING A heart-led leader was a man named Anthony D'Aquanni. Anthony was a hair stylist in White Plains, New York, just across the Hudson River from my hometown, Suffern. Anthony wasn't wealthy, and he didn't have a high-profile public career. He spent much of his life as the owner of a small business that he and his wife, Helen, opened not long after they were married in 1940.

The two of them were seldom apart. For decades, Helen would wash and color the hair of their clients, while Anthony cut and styled. They worked hard, bought a modest home, raised four daughters, and, later, doted on 14 grandchildren. They somehow made every one of them feel like the most special person in the world.

Anthony and Helen never missed a school play or a sporting event or a Scouting ceremony. Their grandchildren grew up watching the two of them hold hands, kiss, laugh, and dance in their kitchen. At Christmas gatherings, Anthony always gave the same toast. "Never forget the three most important things in life," he would say. "Family, family, and family." That was the measure of Anthony's success, the love of his family.

Then one day Helen had a stroke. She survived, but the doctors told Anthony his wife would never walk again. They suggested moving her into a nursing home. The two of them had been married for 55 years, and Anthony couldn't bear the thought of being without the love of his life. So he visited Helen every day and worked tirelessly with her on her physical therapy. He was the first visitor to arrive each morning and the last to leave every night. Eventually the staff gave him his own key. Anthony was the only non-employee in the nursing home's history who could come and go as he pleased.

After months of determined effort, he proved the doctors wrong. Helen walked again.

Their elation was short-lived, however. Three months later, his wife suffered a second stroke. Helen never walked or talked again. But, remarkably, if anyone sang "You Are My Sunshine" to her, she was able to sing along. It was, after all, Anthony's and Helen's song.

Two years after Helen's first stroke, Anthony learned he had an inoperable brain tumor. He died at the age of 82, leaving behind his wife of 57 years (Helen would live to age 89 before passing away).

Before Anthony died, a long string of family members came to say goodbye and to tell him they loved him.

"Everyone keeps *telling me* that they love me," he said to one of his daughters shortly before he died. *"Show me!"*

Those were his very last words: "Show me!"

Don't just tell me you love me, show me. Anthony could utter that message because he had lived it. He had shown Helen he loved her by being present for her every day of his life. He was always there for her, always in tune with what she needed, even in those final years when she could give very little back to him. But his love and devotion were never about what she could give. For Anthony and Helen, it was always about what they could give to others—to their children, their grandchildren, their clients, their friends, their community, and, most of all, each other. That's how you build relationships that last forever.

Through his words and his example, Anthony taught me invaluable lessons about life and leadership. And I was lucky enough to be able to spend many years absorbing these lessons.

That's because Anthony D'Aquanni was my grandfather.

What I admire most about Anthony is that he took what he was given in life and made the absolute most of it. And isn't that what we should all aspire to do? Whether you're the CEO of a Fortune 500 company or the sole proprietor of a small business, an award-winning journalist or the secretary of your church newsletter, an Olympic athlete or a stay-at-home parent, all we can ask of ourselves is that we try to live our lives, at work and at home, as a true expression and reflection of who we are.

My grandfather wasn't wealthy or famous. He didn't have political power and he didn't run a large corporation. But he knew exactly who he was and what he cared about. As he showed me through the way he lived his life, it doesn't matter what titles or awards or accomplishments you've accumulated or placed on your mantel. Success is about building hearts, not resumes. Success fulfills us only when we focus on our passions, when we care as much about others as we do about ourselves. When we lead with our hearts.

Because *who* you are matters.

Rule #45: Do Right

———

"**A**LL WE HAVE ARE OUR HEARTS AND MINDS. IF THESE HEARTS AND minds *aren't* taken care of, what kind of company are we going to be? We need to create an environment where people's hearts and minds can thrive."

That statement, for me, is the epitome of heart-led leadership. It was spoken by the CEO of a billion-dollar company who is committed to growing profits, expanding market share, and satisfying shareholders. A CEO who is committed to accomplishing these things as a heart-led leader.

The individual who said those words to me is Tee Green, one of the most authentic, humble, and service-oriented leaders I've ever met. He is the CEO of Greenway Health, a medical software company based in Carrollton, Georgia. Over the past several years, I have spoken in various venues to the company's executives, employees, and customers and have gotten to know the organization fairly well. Greenway is not just an industry leader in the field of electronic medical records; it is also known for its exceptional service and its caring attitude toward clients, employees, and communities.

I experienced this firsthand when I was at the company's annual conference recently and saw Tee speak to 3,000 Greenway customers. After introducing a new product line, he said: "Look, I'm the CEO. The buck stops here. If anyone here has a problem with our software, or a question about it, call me. Here is my cell phone number."

And Tee then gave his personal cell phone number to the 3,000 attendees. That is putting yourself on the line for your product. That is caring about your customers.

Tee founded Greenway with his father in 1998. The company provides software to physicians, pharmacies, and other health care providers so they can electronically manage medical records and revenue cycles. Greenway also specializes in health care analytics—the use of software to interpret clinical studies, analyze the efficiency of care, or utilize genetic information to develop better treatments. His father is now retired from the firm, but Tee has helped Greenway become one of the country's top providers of medical software. For a while, the company was growing at a rate of 30 percent a year, and although that rate is not sustainable forever, Greenway is still growing rapidly—just last year the company hired 450 new personnel, and now it has 1,700 employees.

Greenway went public in 2012; two years later it was bought for $644 million by Vista Equity Partners, to merge it with Vitera Healthcare Solutions, another medical software company. At the time, Greenway was working with 15,000 health care providers in the United States; Vitera had a client list of 85,000 providers.

Mergers take place all the time in the business world, but there is an aspect of this deal that is not so common: the new company is called Greenway Health, the software products are marketed under the Greenway brand, and the new CEO is none other than Tee Green. Now, how many times do two companies merge and retain the name and the management team of the smaller company? Not often.

When I asked Tee about this, he was his typical humble self. "Well, I think Vista Equity just liked our road map," he said. "They liked where we were driving the company."

But mergers are about hard-nosed business decisions. Even though Vitera was six times the size of Greenway, Vista Equity was not just giving preference to Greenway's products or "book of business." It was buying into the Greenway brand and into Greenway's concept of heart-led leadership. It was buying into the who, not just the what.

I don't have any particular knowledge of medical software, but I am passionate about people and servant leadership. And, based on my experience in working with hundreds of companies and thousands of executives, I can tell you that Greenway is run by some special individuals.

For one, I don't think I've ever been greeted more warmly by staff members at any company than I have been at Greenway. But the distinctiveness of the company's culture goes beyond mere friendliness. It's apparent when you walk into a meeting with Greenway executives how much they care about each other, and that they are dedicated not only to growing their company but also to ensuring that the organization maintains its character for the long term.

"We wanted to build a generational company that would be around for decades and be able to make a true impact," Tee told me. "We wanted to fundamentally change how health care was provided. At the same time, we wanted to attract people who would build a career here, not just stay a few years and move on. I wanted to build an organization that employees would be proud to be a part of.

"Look, anyone can build a company and then sell it a few years later and make a lot of money," he said. "But is that really what it's all about? I'd rather do something for the long term and build something that lasts."

Mike Hairston, executive vice president for sales, and Eric Grunden, vice president for professional services, have worked with Tee for years. Mike first met Tee when they were students and fraternity brothers at Auburn University; he has worked at Greenway almost since its founding in 1999. Eric has been with Greenway for more than a decade. I spoke with the two of them one day in an effort to get more insight into Greenway's brand of heart-led leadership.

Mike shared a story from the company's early days that, to him, symbolizes what Tee and Greenway are all about.

"This happened shortly after I started here. One of the

first sales I made was with a company in Mississippi, and we had some of their employees come to Georgia for training on the new system," he told me. "While they were training, one of the women got a phone call that no parent wants to receive. She found out her son had been killed in a car accident. Well, Tee heard about this and he immediately ran out of his office and went down the hill to the training center so he could console this lady. Then, within an hour, he had somehow secured a private plane to fly her back to Mississippi so she could be with her family.

"Now remember, this is when we were just starting out and Greenway didn't have a lot of staff or financial resources. But Tee felt it was important for us to support this woman in her time of need. Then a week later, he came into my office and said to me, 'I feel like I need to go down to Meridian, Mississippi.' So we went there together and we visited the woman who had lost her son. Tee gave her a long embrace and sat there and talked with her for some time.

"That's the sort of action that comes from the heart of a person. Tee has always had this heart, and it shows in the way he built the company. I believe that companies take on the personality of their leader. If your CEO is brash or dishonest or egocentric, then you wind up with a company that is brash, dishonest, or egocentric. If your CEO has a heart for serving others, then you wind up with a company that has a heart for serving others. And that's what Tee is all about."

Eric Grunden also told me about an incident that illustrates Tee's distinctive style of leadership.

"If you're ever in a meeting with Tee, you see that he uses a whiteboard a lot," Eric said. "And he writes a number down in the corner of the board. So in one of my first meetings with him, I noticed that number on the board and asked him what it was. I guessed that it represented the number of employees at the company. 'You're close,' he told me. 'It's the number of families that are represented by employees who work here.'

"Well, that just says it all about Tee. That sort of caring for the families of his employees. It really hammered home for me that I'd chosen the right company and the right leader to work for."

Mike and Eric told me about what has become known at Greenway as Rule #45: Do Right.

"One time, we came up with a list of 60 or 70 words or phrases that represented what we wanted to be and to achieve as a company," Mike said. "Number 45 on that list was 'do right.' And that has become a phrase that we use all the time now at Greenway. We try to remember Rule #45 because we want to do right by our families, our customers, our co-workers. It's hard sometimes when you're also facing financial pressures to think in these terms, but Tee feels that you should look at everything through the lens of 'Am I doing the right thing?' If you are, then it's the right decision."

Do right. Those two words sum up what Greenway Health is all about. And they are what heart-led leadership is all about.

AS PART OF DOING right, the company has tried to be cognizant of its responsibility to give back to the community. In fact, to me, Tee's greatest success as CEO of Greenway Health isn't in building a billion-dollar company but in fostering a partnership with Rapha Clinics, a nonprofit organization that offers free medical services to people who cannot afford health care.

The first Rapha Clinics were founded in Georgia by Sue Brockman. For years Sue worked on little more than a shoestring budget and a prayer. Tee met Sue in 2012 and discovered that she was managing two medical clinics in Temple and Bowdon, Georgia, with ancient computers and little funding. He believed Rapha's mission of providing free health care to residents living below the poverty line was a perfect way to show Greenway's commitment to giving back and its belief that everyone should have access to quality medical care. So he decided to help. Greenway organized several fund-raisers for Rapha and provided the organization with free medical software and training. The company also recruited volunteers to work at Rapha, looking both among its own employees and among Greenway customers. Some doctors who use the Greenway software now volunteer as staff physicians at the clinics.

"Our customer base is service-oriented," Tee said. "Most physicians go to medical school because they want to help people. So they get excited about things like the Rapha Clinics."

I visited one of these clinics after Tee invited me to speak at Rapha's annual fund-raiser, and I came away incredibly inspired. The clinic, which had several examination rooms for physicians as well as a dental facility, has served about 6,000 patients over the past few years, and not one of them has paid a dime for medical care. What impressed me even more, though, were the passionate volunteers. From the second I walked in the front door, I felt love for the patients in a way that I've never felt in any other doctor's or dentist's office.

"I owe a great deal to Tee and his people," Sue told me. "Tee is such a caring, compassionate person, and he and everyone at Greenway have given so much of their time to support Rapha. And Tee has such a beautiful vision for what Rapha can become."

That vision goes beyond fund-raisers, software, and volunteers for a local health care clinic. Greenway decided to make these clinics a core part of its mission and has set a goal of opening a new Rapha site for every 1,000 new customers. As this book goes to press, two new clinics are slated to open in Georgia and Alabama, and more are in the planning stages. One reason why Greenway employees are so committed to adding those 1,000 new customers is because they know they are doing more than just growing a company. It's not only about making profits; it's also about changing lives.

During my last visit to Greenway's campus, I stayed at

Tee's home. While I was there, I asked him about his management style, his business philosophies, and the culture of the company he built.

"Very early on in my career," he said, "I saw that many people weren't concerned with the heart of the other people they worked with—nobody knew their neighbor, so to speak. But I figured out that if we tried to understand our neighbor, the people we worked with, then we could learn what motivated them and what was in their hearts and minds. And then, once we did that, it had beneficial effects on the whole workplace. People were happier, we had less turnover, and we had more consistency in the execution of our vision."

That sounds great, I told him, but how does a business leader go about accomplishing this?

"Well, that's not to say it's easy," he answered. "It's actually harder this way. Anyone can go into a meeting and be comfortable talking about revenue streams or profit margins. But if you ask someone to talk about themselves, it's uncomfortable. That's a whole other layer there that you're getting into. When you sit down in my office and I ask you what your mind is like, what your heart is like, what is happening with your family, that's uncomfortable, and you have to be a strong and disciplined leader to do it consistently with each of your team members. But it's important if you want to build high-performance teams. Because if you don't understand someone's heart, you won't ever have full trust."

What do you say, I wanted to know, to people who think

this is too touchy-feely to be part of a strategy for business or a leadership philosophy?

"It's true that people may think it's touchy-feely," he said, "but I believe it's just the opposite. Come into my office and ask people about me. No one will say that I'm soft. I look at this as an investment. I'm investing in my team and in their hearts. And the only way to invest in someone's heart is to show them yours."

I did, in fact, ask people in Tee's office about his management style, and they all confirmed that he was a caring but demanding boss. "He is not soft by any means," Mike Hairston told me. "He is very direct in what his expectations are, he is very demanding, and he holds us accountable. But you can require a high level of performance from your team and still be compassionate. Just because you have a great heart doesn't mean you're a pushover."

Near the end of my conversation with Tee, I asked him to tell me about the business principles that he used as the foundation for Greenway Health.

"We're not perfect," he told me, "but what we consider every day is service. We've built our company around the tenets of service, innovation, and leadership. But service is number one. How can we serve? That is what we try to live as a company. Service is when you put others first: your customers, your company, your industry, your community. In corporate America, we're taught to perform, to win. We're taught that it's a dog-eat-dog world. But I like to think that we can win in a different way.

"Every day I wake up and ask myself, 'How can I serve

today? How can I make someone smile? How can I make their day better?' That's the business model I want to have. Because the more you can do that, the more you can positively affect others, the more successful you will be."

How can I serve today? How can I make someone smile? How can I do right? Those are the words of a heart-led leader who happens to be running a billion-dollar company.

The truth is, if Greenway Health can become a billion-dollar company using a model that focuses on taking care of people's hearts and minds and on serving and positively impacting others, other organizations can do the same. Heart-led leadership is not just a warm and fuzzy approach; it's not just an idealistic attitude or a way to make employees and customers happier. It's a leadership philosophy that can positively impact your bottom line. Heart-led leadership is a business model that produces extraordinary love-*driven* results. And why wouldn't everyone want to emulate that?

From the What to the Who

———

THE JOURNEY I TOOK FROM MY GRANDFATHER'S LESSONS IN "WHO you are" to Tee Green's heart-led leadership philosophy was a long one. Although these ideas were obviously a part of my life from the very beginning, it still took me years to truly understand them and to appreciate their importance. The truth is, for much of my early life I was more focused on proving myself than on heart-led leadership. All through high school and college and into my early professional career, I chased the resume, pursued titles and awards, and was addicted to achievement.

As a high school student in Suffern, New York, I was senior class president, an Eagle Scout, and a national award winner in Distributive Education Clubs of America (DECA), which prepares high school students for careers as entrepreneurs and business leaders. I was also involved in a half dozen other school activities or sports teams and was voted the student who did the most for Suffern

High School. My penchant for overachievement followed me to East Carolina University, where I was senior class president, president of my fraternity, and president of the Inter-Fraternity Council; at graduation, I gave the commencement address and was named Most Outstanding Senior.

I chased these achievements in part because of my passion for leadership, but in reality it was more because this is what society expected of me. It's what society expects of all of us—to build a resume.

In retrospect, I can also see that to some degree I relied on these achievements to mask another part of myself—a part of me that was filled with shame and self-doubt, a part of me that I was embarrassed to share with others. As I mentioned earlier, I have dyslexia, which wasn't diagnosed until I was a junior in college, and so I always had a great deal of trouble reading and learning inside the classroom. All through high school and much of college, I just thought I was unintelligent. I constantly tried to hide the fact that I struggled to read, that I was barely skating by academically, or that I attended summer school and special classes for students with learning disabilities.

So I overcompensated. Since it didn't seem likely that I would get into college on my academic record, I learned to pad my resume with other examples of success. And when I discovered that I could be popular and successful based on my personality, work ethic, and ability to lead others, I became hooked on demonstrating my worth through these achievements.

It's not that I *only* focused on achievements or *never* pursued other passions during these years. I was a student and staff member in Up with People, an educational organization that sends young people around the world to perform musical shows, live with host families, and do community service. I also taught conversational English in Japan with the Japanese Exchange and Teaching (JET) Program. For the most part, however, the focus of my life was to pile up as many achievements as I could and then, when I started my professional career, to make as much money as possible.

One day, though, I had an epiphany that made me reconsider the trajectory of my life. An epiphany that made me think again of my grandfather and of the values he had imparted to me. An epiphany that started me on a new journey—a journey that would ultimately lead me to heart-led leadership.

WHEN I WAS 31 years old, I was sleeping on a cot in my office because I could no longer afford my mortgage. I walked everywhere because I couldn't afford a car. I had drained my savings account and sold off almost everything of value that I owned. There were times when I didn't know where my next dollar or my next meal was coming from. It was by far the most stressful and humbling period of my life. And yet, paradoxically, it was also one of the happiest times of my life.

A year earlier I had founded Leader's Challenge, a

nonprofit organization in Denver, Colorado. My vision was to create a high school leadership development program that would engage our youth in community service, servant leadership, and civic responsibility. Since I had commitments of support from some local executives and philanthropists, I signed a lease on an office space, hired a staff, and made the legal arrangements to operate a 501(c)(3) nonprofit. I was confident my efforts were soon going to change the lives of thousands of young people.

Talk about leaping before you look! The commitments of support didn't exactly translate into the raging river of donations I had envisioned. It was more like a trickling stream on a dry riverbed. In retrospect, that's not such a surprise. Regardless of the merit of my vision, I was still operating a start-up, after all. Most donors want to see some measure of success before they write a check. But by the time this realization hit home, I was ensconced in an office and responsible for a seven-person staff, including my younger sister and several close friends who had uprooted their lives to move to Colorado to work for me.

It took less than a year for the financial walls to close in. When it became obvious that the books weren't going to balance, I made some hard decisions. I laid off nearly my entire staff and helped them find other jobs. I sublet my condominium, moved a cot into my office, took my car off the road, and started walking and taking public transportation. I emptied my savings account, sold most of my belongings, and even resorted to borrowing money from my mother and stepfather for living expenses. My business was deep in debt, and I was on the verge of bankruptcy.

During this time, I had many sleepless nights when I stared at the office ceiling from my cot and wondered if I had damaged my career and ruined my life. But I still had faith in my vision, and I refused to give up on it. I knew that I needed to find a way to make Leader's Challenge work. So, with no home to go back to at night and no personal life to speak of, I persevered. When you live in your office, it's not hard to work 90 to 100 hours a week.

Despite my initial missteps and the seeming hopelessness of my efforts, though, I felt strangely fulfilled. That's because, for the first time in my life, I had chosen to make decisions based on who I was as a person and what was in my heart, rather than on what I thought I was supposed to achieve.

I couldn't know for sure that my vision or my long hours of work would pay off, but I knew why I felt fulfilled. My sense of inner peace stood in sharp contrast to the life I'd been living just two years earlier, one that had been far more lucrative financially but less satisfying to me on a personal level.

Back then, fresh out of business school, I had taken a position with the Lotus Development Corporation in Boston as its business partner sales manager for the Northeast. Since IBM owned Lotus, my job involved working with IBM's business partners in Boston, New York, and Philadelphia to sell them Lotus Notes and help them integrate the software with their businesses. It was a well-paying position, one that enabled me to buy an upscale penthouse condo in the city's South End, dress in stylish clothes, and buy an expensive Rolex.

In many ways, I was living my dream, one that I had nurtured since high school. So I was surprised as I went about my life to realize that I was harboring a deep sense of unease.

I was a successful salesman, but mostly because I'm good at building relationships. I wasn't proficient at the technical part of my work, however, because I didn't really understand software or speak that language. And I wasn't even interested in learning more about it because I had no passion for technology or software.

It's fair to ask what I was doing in that position if I wasn't enthusiastic about the product I was selling. The answer is pretty simple: when I was looking for a job, Lotus offered me the most money. After graduating with an MBA from Bond University in Australia, I received offers from several companies, including National Geographic and Johnson & Johnson. The National Geographic position was a great fit for me given my love for history and travel. If I had listened to my heart, I likely would have accepted it.

But it didn't occur to me to listen to my heart.

The bottom line was that no other company could match the signing bonus, base salary, and potential commissions that Lotus put on the table. In my mind, the most money equaled the most success and so I jumped at the offer. But I soon awoke to the realization that I had constructed my life around other people's notions of success.

That epiphany occurred one day as dollar bills rained down on my head—literally. I was attending a sales conference at the Walt Disney World Swan and Dolphin Resort in Orlando with other Lotus and IBM executives when the vice president of sales gave a motivational speech that fired everyone up. At the end of the speech, his voice rose as he made his final pitch. If you sell more products and improve your market share, he practically shouted at us, you will make more money.

You will make more money!

You will make more money!

The refrain echoed around the room as people stood and cheered. Then, as if by magic, thousands of dollar bills rained down on us from the ceiling. It was like a cascade of balloons at the end of a political convention, and it drove the Lotus sales crowd into a frenzy. People with six-figure incomes began pushing and grabbing madly for the bills, as if their family's livelihood depended on it.

I stood there awed by the spectacle, but I couldn't bring myself to join in. All I could do was stand quietly amid the clamor and try to make sense of an unsettling feeling that had come over me. At that moment I realized with surprising certainty that I was living a lie and that my job had very little to do with the person I was inside.

It's not that I resented my fellow salespeople for wanting to make money. I wanted the same thing. And it's not that my life was unhappy. Again, in many ways I was living my dream. But that torrent of cash helped to crystallize the disconnect between the life I was living and the life I thought I should be living. I'd always been passionate about relationships and service to others, about making a difference in the world, but I had chosen a career solely for the material rewards it offered. I had built my life around what I thought I wanted instead of who I was as a person. I had listened to my head and ignored my heart.

Many of us do the same thing every day of our lives without even thinking about it because that's what we're conditioned to do. We live in a "what"-driven society. When we're young, people ask us, "What do you want to be when you grow up?" or "What college do you want to attend?" Our lives and careers are buried in a blizzard of such questions. What is your GPA? What is your SAT/ACT score? What do you do for a living? What is your job title? What neighborhood do you live in? What car do you drive? What is your salary? Once we answer those "what" questions, we think we've got life figured out. But then we wake up and realize that we had the questions backward. Instead of beginning with the what, we should have started with the who.

Who am I? Who do I serve and impact? Who do I love? Who do I want my children to grow up to be? Or, if you're running a business: Who are my clients and my employees? How do I want them to perceive me and my organization? In the long run, the answers to these "who" questions will matter more to us than the answers to the "what" questions. These are the "who" questions that my grandfather Anthony D'Aquanni would no doubt have been asking himself.

Once I understood this and looked more deeply into myself, I realized that I've always wanted to use my gift for building relationships to serve others. I thought back to my time in Up with People and with the JET Program. Those years of traveling internationally, interacting with people from other cultures, and engaging in community service activities had been some of the most fulfilling years of my life. I wanted to reconnect with those core passions.

So I resigned from Lotus and accepted a job as the director of corporate relations at Up with People. I sold my home and moved to Denver. Although I took a huge pay cut, I feel as if my life (and my journey to heart-led leadership) really began when that moving truck pulled up to the curb outside my Boston condo.

Ironically, that position lasted only a year. But without that career change I wouldn't have had the inspiration to found Leader's Challenge. And, yes, that venture got off to a rocky start, but my persistence paid off. Within five years, with the help of my business partner, Joel Mauney, and many generous donors and volunteers, we established Leader's Challenge as the largest high school leadership program in Colorado. Today, the National Leadership Academy (the successor to Leader's Challenge) is one of the most successful high school leadership programs in the country.

I slept on a cot in my office far longer than I would

have liked, but when we turned the organization around I was finally able to move back into the condo, which I'd been subletting. And through my community work with Leader's Challenge I ended up meeting and marrying the love of my life, Jill. My persistence paid off, yes. But more important, my decision to live my life according to the who—to listen to my heart—paid off.

My life has taken several twists and turns since then. I eventually went back to Up with People as its president and CEO for four years. Now I make my living as a leadership speaker, author, executive coach, and entrepreneur. Although I'm more successful now than I was when I worked for Lotus, it means less to me because I'm not obsessed by it—and because I'm making life decisions based not on what I want but on who I am and who I can serve.

In the end, what I learned from my own personal journey is this: before we can think of becoming heart-led leaders, we need to start by shifting our focus from the what to the who. That is where the 18-inch journey from the head to the heart begins. There is a lot more to heart-led leadership than this one shift in thinking, but every journey has to start somewhere. And it starts with *who we are*.

I believe that I'm still on this journey from the head to the heart. I'm still learning about heart-led leadership. But I want to share with you what I have learned so far, because I believe it can transform your life and your organization. We don't have to choose between success and fulfillment in our lives, and we don't have to choose between profits and purpose in our businesses. I know this is true because

I've seen it—hundreds of times. I already introduced you
to Tee Green, who taught me what heart-led leadership
could accomplish in a business environment. Now I'd like
you to meet another special individual, one who showed
me how the power of heart-led leadership could have an
extraordinary impact on thousands of lives in an entirely
different way.

The Heart of Texas

GROVE NORWOOD IS A WHO LEADER WHO INSTINCTIVELY UNDER-stands the importance of heart-led leadership. That is why, a few years ago on a smoldering hot summer afternoon in south Texas, he decided to drop in to tiny St. Matthew's Church.

He had no idea at the time that his split-second decision would be the start of a story that would eventually encompass death, heartbreak, forgiveness, redemption, love, and hope. He had no idea of the impact his heart-led leadership would have on his community, his state, and his country. He had no idea that his story would change thousands of lives, including mine.

Grove just happened to be driving home from church one Sunday when he noticed a small group of people huddled in the grass parking lot at St. Matthew's. Most of us would have driven on by, but he did what any of us could do: he stopped to investigate.

He soon learned that some of the elderly worshipers were suffering from heat stroke. The temperature outside had topped 100 degrees, but it was worse in the tiny sanctuary because the air conditioner had been stolen, leaving a hole in the wall of the church.

Most of us would have felt sad for the church and gone on our way. But Grove did what any of us could do: he spent $350 on an air conditioner, some chains, and a lock, then headed back to St. Matthew's, where one of the deacons, Ulice Parker, met him to help repair the wall and install the new unit.

Grove Norwood and Ulice Parker lived in the same area around Simonton, Texas, just south of Houston, but they were from radically different worlds. Ulice grew up in the deep woods near the Brazos River and spent much of his life picking cotton by hand. He had a speech impediment that made him hard to understand, but he was known as a hardworking, gentle spirit who had weathered the storms of a harsh life. He was eking out a living as a vegetable gardener when he met Grove Norwood.

As a pilot during the Vietnam War, Grove had been awarded two Silver Stars for valor while helping to rescue troops pinned down by enemy troops. He was a successful brokerage manager with a national insurance company when he met Ulice Parker.

Grove did what any of us could do: he began helping Ulice, his family, and their church in all sorts of ways. When Ulice's roof gave in, Grove helped fix it. When the two men visited with each other, Grove's young son and daughter often played with Ulice's children and grand-children. Grove also bought Ulice's church a new organ and was, as far as anyone knows, the first white person to attend a service there.

In 2000, however, tragedy struck and sent shock waves through Grove's life and his community.

Grove's kids were returning home from a tee-ball prac-tice on April 10, 2000, when his four-year-old daughter, Joy, said she needed to go to the bathroom. After Joy in-sisted several times that she couldn't wait, her mother agreed to stop on the isolated two-lane country road they were traveling.

It was dusk when they pulled over on the opposite side of the road, where the shoulder was wide enough to park their van. Not knowing what side of the road they were on, however, Joy popped open the passenger-side door and jumped out—right into the path of an oncoming vehicle. The vehicle that hit Joy continued down the road.

Joy died at the scene of the accident.

Everyone was devastated. Grove was consumed by a grief he never could have imagined, and the community demanded justice for the driver who had fled.

At the crime scene, the police found a broken piece of plastic from the front of the vehicle that had struck Joy. This became a key piece of evidence as they began search-ing for the vehicle and its driver.

A few days later, the police found the vehicle and its owner—Ulice Parker.

On the night of the accident, Ulice Parker was 68 years

old. He wore thick glasses to correct deteriorating vision and, to state the obvious, shouldn't have been driving. When the police questioned him, he said he had no idea he had hit Joy. He was devastated to learn he was responsible for the death of his close friend's daughter.

As a father, I don't think I could forgive someone who ran over and killed my nine-year-old daughter, Caroline. But Grove Norwood is a better man than I am. He did what any of us could do: he forgave.

When he learned Ulice had accidentally killed his daughter, Grove drove to Ulice's home to console him. The two men prayed, and Grove forgave his friend. Then he invited Ulice and his wife, Carrie, to attend Joy's funeral. Because the couple was extremely poor and didn't own clothes to wear to the service, Grove bought them suitable clothes to wear that day. Then they all sat together, side by side, as they said their goodbyes to Joy and buried her.

The people in and around Simonton, Texas, couldn't believe what Grove had done. There stood Grove Norwood, on the day he was burying his precious four-year-old daughter, arm in arm with the man who had caused her death. This act of forgiveness changed the fabric of the town. This act of empathy helped teach the community, and the world, the true meaning of love.

Six months later, Grove appeared before a grand jury in Austin County, Texas, and did what any of us could do: he appealed to the jury to not indict Ulice Parker for a criminal motor vehicle offense. The judge and the jury took Grove's words to heart and Ulice remained a free man.

A month after that, Grove and the members of his church decided to build a new home for the Parker family. Grove not only forgave Ulice for accidentally killing his daughter, bought him a suit for the funeral, and worked to keep him out of jail, but also helped build him and his wife a new home!

I first learned of Grove's story from Rusty Gilmore, a sales rep in the restaurant industry who had attended one of my speeches. Rusty approached me after my talk and we visited for a few minutes. He told me my message had reminded him of a friend of his, Grove Norwood; he asked if he could send me a video about Grove's incredible story.

So Rusty mailed me a copy of *The Heart of Texas*, an award-winning documentary that told the story of Grove Norwood and Ulice Parker, which I just recounted for you here. The first time I watched it was on my laptop during a flight back to Colorado. I felt sorry for the gentleman sitting next to me on the plane, because I was crying uncontrollably by the time I'd finished the video. It moved me in a thousand ways.

So I did what any of us could do: I bought a hundred copies of the video and mailed them to close friends. Then I called Grove and asked him if we could meet. I wanted to learn as much from him as possible about what it means to lead from the heart.

Grove Norwood has impacted thousands of people through his story of forgiveness, but his story didn't end with the forgiveness of Ulice Parker. His impact as a heart-led leader goes much further and much deeper.

Countless people have seen *The Heart of Texas*, and I can't imagine that anyone who saw the documentary wasn't moved by it. Some of them took the next step, as I did, and passed the documentary along. Some sent Grove a note or donated to his foundation. And some acted on what they saw and what they felt.

Burl Cain, the warden at the state penitentiary in Angola, Louisiana, was among those who watched *The Heart of Texas* and acted on it. Burl took over at Angola in 1995, when it was known as the bloodiest, most dangerous prison in America. Since then, he has used heart-led leadership to build a culture of love and trust among the most untrustworthy men and women society has to offer. Among his innovations was to open a seminary inside the prison, run by the New Orleans Baptist Theological Seminary. To date, nearly 250 inmates have received four-year degrees from the seminary and become pastors who minister to other prisoners. More than a third of the 6,500 inmates now worship regularly at one of the prison's 25 official denominational churches. There are 400 or so religious services or faith-based study programs offered each month, not only for various Christian faiths but also for Muslim and Jewish prisoners. Other initiatives have included an in-prison hospice, where prisoners care for dying inmates, and the Malachi Dads project, where prisoners pledge to provide spiritual leadership for their kids in an effort to break the cycle of crime that often plagues several generations of a family.

As a result of such programs, Angola has been transformed and today is one of the safest prisons in America, even though the majority of inmates either are on death row, are serving a sentence of life without parole, or have such a long sentence that they are effectively in prison for life. Incidents of inmate violence dropped 70 percent over 15 years, and numerous prisoners can now earn the right to work in public settings, such as cooking or cleaning in staff residences or interacting with the public during the prison's annual rodeos, which attract 70,000 attendees each year. Although punishment is still harsh for those inmates who don't follow the rules, Burl Cain believes the culture of the prison has been transformed by these initiatives because they provide a sense of purpose to prisoners who know they either are going to die or are going to spend much of their lives behind bars.

As a part of his commitment to heart-led leadership, Burl began showing *The Heart of Texas* in his prison so that inmates could see and hear Grove's story of love and forgiveness. Soon inmates across Louisiana and Texas were asking to hear more about Grove and his story. After being contacted by some wardens, Grove began speaking in prisons. Over time, he realized that much of the interest in his story could be traced back to Warden Burl Cain at the Louisiana State Penitentiary.

So Grove did what Who Leaders do: he acted.

Grove contacted Burl and asked if they could speak. He learned about the seminary that Burl had founded at Angola and was told that the prisoners who completed their degree and became ministers were becoming agents of positive change in the harsh culture of a maximum-security prison. Grove believed he could replicate that model in Texas, and so he founded the Heart of Texas Foundation, which he now runs with his wife, Brenna, and others. In 2010 he partnered with Southwestern Seminary to fund a fully accredited program at the Darrington Unit, a maximum-security prison near Houston. It's currently the only program of its kind in Texas and has the same goal of turning prisoners into ordained ministers who will then provide spiritual guidance and counseling to fellow inmates.

My 18-inch journey took me to that prison and made me more compassionate and changed my life forever. Although it certainly didn't change my mind about the need to imprison individuals who commit crimes, it did help me to understand that some prisoners are good people who made bad choices. And it helped me to see that even hardened criminals can have love in their hearts.

The Darrington Unit is isolated along Farm to Market Road 521 in the middle of more than 6,000 flat acres south of Houston. It's been around for nearly a century and is now home to more than 1,600 prisoners. Most of these men were convicted of violent crimes, and nearly one-sixth of them are serving life sentences. Most people see these prisoners as the unreachable, the unchangeable, the unforgiveable—but not Grove Norwood.

The idea of running a seminary inside a prison seems at first glance like a noble but ultimately futile endeavor. These are convicted murderers, rapists, and armed robbers. How many would be interested in attending a seminary? And of those, how many would even be open to—or capable of—the type of change required by this type of study?

When I talked with Grove and he told me about the prison seminary, I knew that I had to see for myself. I had to experience it. I had to learn from it. I had to make that story, that experience, a part of my own life. So after a speech I gave in San Antonio, I made a side trip to Darrington. Grove and Rusty agreed to escort me into the prison so that I could experience firsthand the hope that this seminary program is creating.

I had visited jails and prisons for volunteer work in the past, but this was my first trip to a maximum-security facility. When we stepped out of the car on a hot, humid Texas morning, my shirt was drenched from perspiration, but I wasn't entirely sure if it was from the heat or from my nerves.

At the first gate, we put our driver's licenses in a bucket and watched as an officer pulled the bucket up by a rope to his watchtower. The officer buzzed us through a series of barbed-wire-topped gates, and then we passed through a metal detector before arriving at what reminded me of a door to a bank safe.

Then the heavy door shut behind us, effectively locking us inside the prison walls. From there, we made our way to the library, where we took a seat across a table from a tall, muscular man who, if it hadn't been for his white prison jumpsuit, could have been mistaken for a wide receiver for a pro football team.

Tracy—prisoner 733709—had been in Darrington for nearly two decades. He had grown up with a loving mother and grandmother, he told us, but had never known his father. This, I discovered, is a recurring theme with inmates. I could see the pain in Tracy's eyes as he told us how much he wished he had known his father. After high school, he started hanging out with a bad crowd, stealing small things here and there. He eventually graduated to bigger crimes, he said, culminating in an armed robbery. Tracy was caught, convicted, and sentenced to 50 years in prison.

When the seminary was launched in 2010, Tracy signed up. Like most prisoners who participate in the seminary program, he wanted to do something positive during his years behind bars, something that would provide a sense of purpose to his life. And over time, he told me, he felt his heart begin to change. Tracy used to be a follower and he used to hang around with the wrong crowd, but the seminary turned him into a model prisoner who now leads others by his positive example. I was told that this was common with most of the seminary students.

Before we said goodbye, I shook Tracy's hand and told him I was proud of him for the efforts he was making to change his life for the better. I gave him a hug, told him he is a good man, and told him that I believe in him.

His response broke my heart.

"If I knew my daddy and he had told me those exact words when I was a teenager," he said, "I probably wouldn't be in prison."

Tracy is one of the many prisoners who have experienced the impact of Grove's heart-led leadership and who, in turn, are trying to demonstrate heart-led leadership to others. These men are changing the culture of their prison. If that type of change is possible in that type of environment, then certainly it's possible in your family, in your organization, and in your community.

But for me, the even bigger lesson to take from Grove Norwood's story isn't about prison rehabilitation. It's about the multiplying impact of heart-led leadership. Grove Norwood and Burl Cain are Who Leaders who acted on the opportunities to live life differently and to make a difference in the world around them. Grove acted when he saw the need at St. Matthew's Church and in the life of Ulice Parker. He acted on the opportunity to forgive. He acted on the opportunity to change the culture of a prison—an opportunity that came about only because Burl Cain himself had acted on the opportunity to share Grove's story.

Heart-led leaders are always looking for that "something more." I could have been satisfied with the lessons on forgiveness and the warm, fuzzy feeling that I got from watching the documentary about Grove, but I would have missed the full effect of the learning experience that awaited me. Not only would I have missed out on the impact it made on my own life and my own thinking but, more important, I would have missed out on the impact I can now make on the lives of others as a result of what I learned from Grove.

Seven months after I visited Darrington, I took a small group of friends from Colorado to meet with Burl Cain at the state penitentiary in Angola, Louisiana. Not for a sightseeing tour, but because Grove wants to help launch a prison seminary program in Colorado and we want to help him. Burl Cain has created a model that Grove is replicating in Texas and that we hope, in turn, to help him replicate in Colorado.

During my visit to Angola, I stayed overnight at the warden's guest home on the prison grounds and had dinner with Burl Cain. The meal was cooked by inmates, and I was able to interact with these men, many of whom had committed murder or other violent crimes and were in prison for life. I found them to be personable, respectful individuals who had made a terrible mistake before their incarceration and were now trying to make the best of life in prison. Burl struck me as a tough man who expects inmates to toe the line but who also believes in treating individuals with love and respect and in giving prisoners the opportunity to rehabilitate themselves and to find a purpose for their lives.

That visit to Angola is just one of the ways that my life has been impacted since I first heard Grove's story. He showed me that when a leader's heart is full of love and service toward others, organizations will thrive and communities can change. He challenged me to become a better man. He inspired me to be a better husband and father. And he opened my heart to the power of forgiveness. Above all, Grove taught me that if you can change a criminal's heart, you can change prison itself. And if you can change a community's heart, even one behind bars, you can change the world. That's the power of heart-led leadership.

PART TWO

THE 18-INCH JOURNEY

From the Head to the Heart

I WAS 10 YEARS OLD AND ON A FIFTH-GRADE FIELD TRIP THE FIRST TIME I needed stitches. We were hiking at Kakiat Park in Rockland County, New York, when I tripped on a sharp rock and split the bottom of my right palm trying to break my fall.

There was blood everywhere. My mom rushed me to Good Samaritan Hospital, and I had to get two shots and eight stitches. I cried like a five-year-old. I was so distraught that the doctor allowed my mother to hold my hand during the procedure. And that is when my mother whispered to me the most loving words I've ever heard: "If I could take all of your pain for you, Tommy, I would."

I never really understood the magnitude of those words until I became a parent 26 years later. To me, the unconditional love we give our children is the purest and deepest form of love there is. *If I could take all of your pain for you, I would.*

There is a reason, of course, that parents act so instinctively from a place of unconditional love toward their children. It's because they are responding with their hearts, not their heads. So my question is this: How would our lives, our organizations, and our communities look if we responded to every person and to every situation with our hearts rather than with our heads?

That is the goal of heart-led leadership.

It's true that the love we feel for our children is not the same as what we typically feel for friends, colleagues, clients, or co-workers. But genuine heart-led leaders act from a place of love in everything they do—not just at home with family but at work and in their communities. My friend Steve Farber, a best-selling author and founder of the Extreme Leadership Institute, puts it this way: "When you look up *love* in the dictionary," he says, "there isn't an asterisk next to the word. It doesn't say, 'Not applicable between 9 and 5 on Monday through Friday.' "

Part Two of this book is about love and leadership. It's about the 18-inch journey from your head to your heart. It's about meeting other heart-led leaders who have taken this journey and learning from them.

I've devoted my career to studying leadership. Aside from my family, it's my passion in life. In my career as a speaker, author, entrepreneur, CEO, and executive coach, I've met thousands of leaders. In all of my conversations with them, I've discovered, as I noted in the introduction, that the most successful leaders are those who lead with love in their hearts.

Leadership styles have evolved in the past few decades. The biggest shift has been a move from the old-school traits that we have traditionally been taught to value, such as authoritativeness, strategic thinking, and bottom-line decision making, to a greater emphasis on humility, vulnerability, transparency, selflessness, and authenticity. The old-school leadership style is often referred to as "command and control," but that approach is increasingly becoming less common in corporate America, and even in the military. It's not that old-school skills aren't important; it's just that there is much more to successful leadership today.

More leaders are recognizing that they need to lead from a sense of compassion and genuine concern for the lives and careers of those who work for them. And the people we lead, especially those in the younger generation, value and gravitate toward leaders who care about who they are. So the values that drive and validate us at home—things like the deep empathy of a mother or the desire and focus a father feels to help his child succeed—aren't checked outside the office door.

Heart-led leadership doesn't mean becoming a touchy-feely manager or executive who hugs colleagues or tears up at meetings. What it does mean is acting from a place of understanding, generosity, compassión, and empathy for those you lead. Why? Because our ability to lead is directly correlated to our ability to connect to the hearts and minds of those we wish to lead.

The distance from your head to your heart is not long.

It's always been amazing to me that we can land a man on the moon nearly 240,000 miles away or send a satellite hurtling more than 12 billion miles into the farthest reaches of our solar system, and yet most of us have enormous difficulty in traveling those 18 metaphorical inches in our daily lives. For years we've been focused on the six inches between our ears. But the 18 inches between the head and the heart, between our intellect and our emotions, is even more important.

I believe in this so passionately that I co-founded the Center for Heart-Led Leadership and created a one-year leadership development program to teach senior leaders the skills and values of leading from the heart. I also co-founded the Brooks & Spaulding speaker management company, which represents some of the most successful heart-led thought leaders in the country.

My goal in these endeavors is to abolish the distinction between hard and soft management and leadership skills. What business schools and traditionalists have often dismissed as "soft" skills or people skills are, in fact, often the most important skills a leader can possess. And they are skills all of us can develop and use, regardless of our background, personality, or position.

If you'll commit to embarking on this journey, I believe it will revolutionize how you think of leadership and managing others. In the chapters that follow, I'm going to share some of the lessons I've learned about this journey from the head to the heart. Many of the lessons you'll read about are drawn from heart-led leaders who have shaped my own life and career over the years. They have proven to be incredible teachers in showing me the power of *who you are*. Each of the chapters represents a step—an "inch"—in the heart-led leadership journey that will change your life. I believe it will reshape your organization and the lives of everyone around you. I'm hoping you will come away with as much from these stories as I have—and, more important, that you will pass these lessons on to others.

1. Tragedy to Triumph: A Culture of Love

ON APRIL 20, 1999, SHORTLY AFTER 11:00 A.M., PRINCIPAL FRANK DeAngelis was in his office meeting with a teacher when a secretary rushed in to tell him about reported gunfire at the school. Frank ran into the hallway and saw two young men with guns at the other end of the long main corridor. What happened in the next few moments seemed to occur in slow motion, the scene forever etched in his memory.

He saw explosions of light, heard bullets ricochet off walls, and watched a glass trophy case shatter. He stared at a shotgun pointed in his direction and was certain he was about to die. Then he noticed a group of students in a side hallway and rushed to usher them out of the line of fire. The gunman at that moment inexplicably turned and ran up a staircase.

These were the first chaotic moments of a deadly rampage that shocked the nation and made Columbine High School synonymous with school shootings. By the time the guns were silenced that day, two high school students, Eric Harris and Dylan Klebold, had murdered 13 people before taking their own lives. Twenty-one other people were injured. One of those who died was Dave Sanders, a business teacher, a basketball coach, and Frank's best friend. He was the teacher the gunman chased up the stairwell, mysteriously sparing Frank's life.

In the weeks and months that followed, Frank grieved and cried with the rest of the Columbine community at funerals and memorial services. He grappled with survivor's guilt over the fact that the gunman had pursued his friend rather than firing at him. He suffered from post-traumatic stress disorder, and from chest pains that sent him to the emergency room. Most of all, however, he wondered where he had gone wrong. He stayed up nights, haunted by the knowledge that two students at his school had murdered their peers.

By the time of the shootings, Frank DeAngelis had already spent two decades at Columbine, as a history teacher, baseball coach, assistant principal, and principal. He was an expressive person who loved his job and was proud of his efforts to interact with staff and students. He walked the hallways every day, hung out in the cafeteria to talk with students, and popped into classrooms to chat. After the tragedy he realized that, despite these efforts, two students had still felt so unaccepted and unloved that they'd committed this horrific massacre. If there were two, there could be two more. Frank knew deep inside that somehow he needed to change the culture of his school.

He responded to the shootings by asking the student body to help him rebuild the school and restore a sense of community. He promised that he wouldn't quit his post until everyone then in high school had graduated. When those freshmen graduated in 2002, Frank made another promise, this one to himself. Realizing that his work wasn't done, he committed to himself to stay on the job until all the children who were in kindergarten in 1999 had also graduated from high school. In 2012, with Frank DeAngelis at the helm, Columbine graduated the class of seniors who had been kindergarteners at the time of the tragedy. I had the honor of speaking to the class of 2012; it was a moment that I will never forget. Two years later, in 2014, Frank finally retired as principal of Columbine High School, after a 35-year career in education.

In the 15 years between the tragedy and his retirement, Frank helped transform the site of one of America's darkest moments into a beacon of light, hope, and promise. He did it by making a commitment to always act out of love, and to teach his students and staff to do the same.

I've visited Columbine High School many times to see my friend Frank or to speak to his students. And I'll tell you, I've never been inside a public high school like Columbine, where you can smell, feel, and taste acceptance and grace in every corner of the building. Walking the halls between classes with Frank is an experience unlike any I've ever had. Students continually call out, "Hey, Mr.

D!" Frank knows almost everyone by name. He gives hugs, knuckles, and high-fives. He stops to talk to students about their schoolwork and their personal lives. He quizzes them about what they're learning. He encourages them. He breathes love into each and every student and teacher. He introduces me to staff members who, unprompted, tell me, "That man is the real deal. He's changed this school."

Frank isn't perfect, as he'll quickly tell you. The Columbine massacre took a toll on his personal life and health. His marriage ended. He received death threats. He suffered from depression. But he never gave up.

"The tragedy was a wake-up call," he says. "I always cared for my students, but I learned that there were some who still didn't feel part of the family. So I said, 'If we're going to change the culture of this school, we have to make sure that every person feels loved and feels valued. Every student, every teacher, every secretary, every janitor.' It wasn't easy. It took a lot of work. I sat down with countless groups of students to ask them what we could do better. The honor students and the at-risk kids. The athletes and the skateboarders. The chess club and the drama club. Everyone. Because how do you make everybody in every group feel a part of the school community? That's what I wanted to know. How do you show love to all students?"

Frank continued to wander the halls and the classrooms, just as he had always done. He still tried to attend every school or sporting event that fit into his schedule. But he began to understand that while setting a personal example is important, it wasn't enough. So he implemented other practices to help students feel a sense of belonging. School assemblies, for instance, became models of inclusiveness. Instead of merely recognizing athletic teams or academic performers, these events included skateboarding shows, drama sketches, rap-offs, and other routines that helped give every student a connection to the Columbine community.

One of his most successful ideas was to string 1,700 carabiners (the metal spring-loaded clips that are used to secure rock-climbing ropes) into a long chain and hang it on the wall in the main corridor of the school. He introduced the idea at a student assembly, where he handed a carabiner to every student, and then talked about how the unique skills and gifts of each individual needed to be merged to form a stronger, more cohesive whole. He asked the students to loop their carabiners together in one long strand, and to consider how every person represented a link in the "We Are Columbine" chain. He began an annual practice of handing carabiners from the chain to all the graduating students as a reminder of their place in the Columbine family. Then, at the start of the next school year, he would hand out new carabiners to incoming freshmen and have them add their links to a new chain.

"It's all about making people feel like part of a family," Frank says. "And it starts with love. Because people don't give a damn how much you know until they know how much you care."

And Frank DeAngelis cares. His actions and intentions are driven by a burning desire to make everyone feel valued and loved. In fact, every single time I hear from him, whether it's by phone, email, or text, he tells me that he loves me. I often joke with Frank that he says he loves me more than my own wife does!

At school, he always put extra time in his schedule to spend with at-risk kids because, as he says, "it's easy to love and help the 4.0 students whom you know are going to college. But there are other kids out there who need someone to look them in the eye and say, 'I love you. You're important.' To give them hope." He sent handwritten Christmas cards every December to each of his 150 staff members, in addition to notes throughout the year to congratulate people on an achievement or to thank them for their dedication to education. And when he wandered the cafeteria at lunchtime, he frequently picked up a mop to keep the floor clean.

"When people would see me doing that, they'd say, 'Wait, you're the principal. What are you doing?' And I'd tell them, 'I want a clean environment for you to learn in.' So then I'd see students start to pick up mops or clean up trash. It spreads."

Individually, these are small actions. None of them on their own is enough to truly impact the culture of the school. But collectively they create change.

"Ultimately, it's not about having a system," Frank says. "You want to build a culture where people run through walls for each other, not set up a system. It's not about having tougher policies at school. It's really about making an environment that kids want to be in. When they want to be in class, when they want to learn, then the other problems start to go away. Our students aren't here just to learn math, science, and English. They're learning about life. They're learning about leadership. And love is at the core of leadership."

INCH #1: LOVE

Love can reveal itself in the simplest of ways—by giving someone hope or telling a person that he or she is important. If love can turn around the culture of a public school with nearly 2,000 students and staff members, why can't the same thing happen at your company or organization?

2. What's Hanging on Your Walls?

———

FOR TWO DECADES, ROD DIXON WAS ONE OF THE WORLD'S GREATEST athletes. He represented New Zealand three times in the Olympic Games, and in the early 1980s he was the top-ranked runner on the competitive American road-racing circuit. His Olympic accomplishments include a bronze medal in the 1,500 meters at the 1972 Munich Olympics, a fourth-place finish in the 5,000 meters at the 1976 Montreal Games, and a tenth-place showing in the marathon at the 1984 Los Angeles Olympics. In between these Olympian achievements, Rod Dixon proved himself to be one of the most versatile and successful distance runners of all time, with a victory in the New York City Marathon in 1983, two bronze medals in the world cross-country championships, and wins in such prestigious road races as the Falmouth Road Race on Cape Cod, the Bay to Breakers race in San Francisco, and the Philadelphia Half-Marathon.

In 1997 I was living on the Gold Coast of Australia

while attending business school at Bond University. During one of my semester breaks I visited New Zealand, where I spent three weeks backpacking through that picturesque country. Before my trip, one of my mentors told me that I should work in a visit with an old friend of his, Rod Dixon, who lived in Nelson, New Zealand. He told me about Rod's accomplishments and suggested that I go for a run with him. So after landing in New Zealand I called Rod. When I told him that I was reaching out to him at the suggestion of a mutual friend, he not only agreed to meet me but graciously invited me to spend the night at his home. I was about to learn an important lesson about heart-led leadership.

After settling into Rod's home, I asked him if he wanted to go for an afternoon run. I was 26 years old. Rod was 47 and retired from competitive racing. I had dreams of outrunning the former Olympian, who I was sure had to be well past his prime running years. And for the first half-hour of our run together, I thought I was on the verge of doing just that. But then came the hill, a very long hill where Rod began sprinting away from me with astonishing ease. I tried so hard to reel him back in that I pushed my body beyond what I was capable of. As I gasped for breath and stumbled my way to the top, I threw up in the middle of a run for the first time in my life.

Later, after I had staggered home, showered, and recovered a bit, Rod gave me a tour of his beautiful house and introduced me to his family. Then we went to a local pub for dinner. It was a wonderful evening. But I could barely finish my meal; I had lost my stomach somewhere back on that seemingly endless incline.

Over dinner Rod talked about his family, about growing up in New Zealand, and about how much he loved his ranch. He talked about anything and everything except his legendary running career. Not once did he mention the Olympics or any of his other races. The following morning, before I headed out to see more of New Zealand, Rod took me for a drive in his beat-up old Ford pickup truck. As we chatted, I asked him the question that had been on my mind since the previous night.

"Rod, why don't you have any of your Olympic medals or awards, or even pictures of your running career, in your home?" I asked him. "I didn't see anything on your walls about your achievements. Is there a reason you don't talk about it?"

"I keep all that stuff in a box up in the attic," Rod said to me in a soft voice.

"Man, if I had won an Olympic medal or the New York City Marathon, those puppies would be hanging above my fireplace or on the wall of my office," I mused.

Rod Dixon then told me something that I've never forgotten.

"I'm not defined by my medals and my accomplishments, Tommy," he said. "I'm defined by the people who love me and those I love and serve in return."

I travel to more than 100 cities a year. Between my tenure as the CEO of Up with People and my years crisscrossing the country on the speaking circuit, I have visited countless corporate headquarters, private homes, and places of work. I have had the privilege of meeting and working with thousands of individuals, from world leaders to high school principals, from sales managers to front-line managers. But I have never, ever met anyone as humble as Rod Dixon.

Normally, the signs of executives' egos are hung on the walls, on full display. Pictures of people with famous politicians. Awards, plaques, and trophies. Framed graduation certificates. All of it showcased proudly, at home or at the office. At one point in my life I was the same way. My walls were full of everything that could tell the world how successful I was. My motto was, "If I won it, I hung it!" The local frame shop knew me by name.

But Rod Dixon taught me about the value of humility. He taught me that when you have a strong sense of who you are, you don't need to define yourself by your accomplishments. Today, my office is filled with pictures of my wife and children. I no longer display anything in my home or my office that showcases my accomplishments. I would rather be defined by those I love and serve.

Now, I don't mean to imply you are a lesser person if you hang your graduation certificate or graduate degree in your office or proudly display an award you've received. I don't want to begrudge anyone the chance to display some of their accomplishments. But I do think it's important that we recognize these awards, trophies, and certificates for what they actually are. They represent the what in our lives and not the who. They represent what we have done, not who we are. Yes, visitors can tell a lot about a person by what he or she has hanging on the walls. But I would argue that sometimes you can tell even more by what is not hanging there.

INCH #2: HUMILITY

Humility begins and ends with four magical words: It's not about you. It isn't about deflecting compliments or projecting false modesty—it's about demonstrating that whom you love, whom you care about, and whom you lead is more important than what you accomplish. Rick Warren wrote in *The Purpose Driven Life*, "True humility is not thinking less of yourself; it is thinking of yourself less."

3. Dare to Care

IMAGINE DEALING WITH THE DEATH OF YOUR FATHER AFTER YOUR OWN multiyear battle with breast cancer. Imagine believing that you're at the pinnacle of your career when your boss calls you in for a meeting and then unexpectedly fires you for not delivering the results he had expected. How do you recover from that kind of devastation?

For Cheryl Bachelder, the answer, initially, was to semiretire, do some board work (Cheryl and I serve on a nonprofit board together), and spend some time reconsidering her goals. Was it time to go down an entirely different road? she wondered. Maybe even get off the corporate career track entirely?

Given some time to think, Cheryl concluded that "my gifts are in business leadership." She decided she wanted to go back into the business world. But she wanted to be a different kind of leader.

"Business leaders have a huge opportunity to influence people's lives," she said. "I wanted to have a purpose."

Before long, Cheryl found herself sitting in another corner office, this time as the CEO of her former company's biggest rival.

Well, *rival* might be a pretty strong word, since her new employer, Popeyes Louisiana Kitchen (popularly known as "Popeyes Chicken"), wasn't performing all that well. Guest traffic was declining. Same-store sales were negative. Unit volume and profitability were dangerously low. There were no new products in the pipeline. The stock price had fallen from $34 to $13. Popeyes was a disaster in the making.

Cheryl's faith in her leadership abilities had been shaken by her earlier firing. She had come up through the ranks at four Fortune 500 companies and had always excelled. She now realized, though, that she had an opportunity to grow as a leader. So instead of doing things the way she had always done them, and instead of following the example of her previous bosses, she decided to craft a new leadership model for herself and her team.

There would be no more demeaning of employees, she decided, and no actions that would make people feel like mere cogs in a machine. Her goal was to find ways to lift people up, unearth their strongest skills, help them discover their purpose, and urge them to become partners in achieving the company's mission. But Cheryl's most important decision may have been to step out of the spotlight and let her team lead. She decided that her role was to support her team members and empower their vision.

Asked to sum up this new philosophy, Cheryl said simply: "I wanted to give people dignity."

What followed was nothing short of a business miracle. Emboldened by Cheryl, her team soon came up with an idea to turn their business model upside down and do things that hadn't been done before in the franchise business.

Their first bold move came after deciding they were focusing their efforts in the wrong place. Most franchise organizations focus on the end user—the customer who shells out cash for a meal. Franchisors survey them, focus-group them, test-kitchen them, coddle them, and then rail at the franchisees and front-line employees about every customer whim that needs to be satisfied. The result is that franchisors and franchisees are often at one another's throats. If corporate procedures aren't followed, the franchisor may threaten to pull the franchisee's license. On the other hand, franchisees frequently complain that the corporate office never delivers on promises of product or marketing support.

Cheryl's team at Popeyes decided to do it differently. They chose to focus first on the well-being and profitability of the franchisee. Their assumption was that if they took care of the people who had invested their own hard-earned money in the enterprise, then the local owners would in turn take care of customers. After all, the franchisee has the most to lose if customers aren't happy.

As part of this effort, Cheryl's team decided to start by getting to know every single franchisee one-on-one, as people. They took time to visit restaurants and meet the owners. They asked them about their lives, their families, and their goals. They asked them for their business opinions and their feedback. As one team member put it: "If you are in the franchising business, you should love the franchisees."

Their next quest was to maximize the efficiency of advertising dollars. At the time, advertising was controlled by local owners. The Popeyes executives, however, believed that advertising decisions made from the home office would produce better results. So they convened a meeting to convince franchisees they'd get more bang for their buck if advertising was managed by corporate headquarters. After the senior team presented its case, the franchisee representatives asked for time to discuss the proposal privately.

When the executives were called back into the room, the franchisees presented them with a challenge. They would go along with the new plan, they said, but only if corporate had a real stake in the outcome. They asked for $6 million in additional advertising funds from Popeyes!

Just to be clear, advertising funds in a franchise organization typically come from the revenues earned by franchisees. Most franchisors don't pay for advertising. So the franchisees were laying down a challenge to the new leadership team: *If you really believe this is the right thing to do, put your money where your mouth is. If we put our businesses on the line with this move, then we want your careers on the line as well.*

Cheryl's team took the idea to the board of directors and sold it. Headquarters and the franchisees would be joined at the hip. They would succeed or fail together. Now, you know I wouldn't be telling you this story if they had failed, but what is impressive is just how spectacularly they succeeded.

This was the first of numerous initiatives during Cheryl's tenure as CEO where Popeyes needed franchisees to get on board with a business plan. In every instance, if any franchisees felt they couldn't give their backing to an initiative—either because they didn't understand it or because they sincerely felt it was the wrong decision—the Popeyes team slowed down before moving on. They decided that a mutual understanding between headquarters and local owners was essential. Relationships with franchisees always took priority. How many leadership teams are willing to do that?

Cheryl also transformed the way she dealt with her own team and direct reports. Do you want to know how the CEO of one of the fastest-growing franchises in the world now spends her time each week? Serving. Every Monday and Tuesday is dedicated to coaching her staff. She spends one and a half hours every two weeks in individual meetings with her direct reports. Let me repeat that. The CEO of a publicly traded Fortune 500 company spends two-fifths of her week coaching direct reports. Why isn't she busier "running the company"? Because she believes that she can best serve the company by serving her team.

"In those meetings, we talk about work, but we also talk about their lives outside of work. It's important to focus on the whole person," Cheryl said. "Every person has value and should be listened to and cared for. I want to take people on a journey to personal purpose, to help them grow, to be the best they can be. That is how you give people dignity. You should love the people you lead."

Cheryl believes that nothing disturbs our soul like the idea of our life being without purpose. So Popeyes now helps staff members develop their own personal purpose statement and even offers a full-day workshop that helps individuals recognize their talents and ways they can use their gifts to help others. In fact, Cheryl wants to change the perception of what it means to work in a fast-food restaurant. She noted that 67 percent of Americans work in the restaurant industry at some point in their life (I worked at McDonald's in high school and Domino's Pizza in college), and she believes it can and should be seen as a positive, purposeful experience.

"I believe we need to create a great environment for people at the restaurant level. If we want guests to be well cared for, then employees also need to be well cared for," she said.

I was curious, though, to know if Cheryl's passion and her commitment to servant leadership really cascaded through the organization. Did any of this actually translate into better treatment for employees and customers?

I got my answer when I saw this quote from one of her restaurant managers in Chicago: "I have the best job ever. I am a teacher, a counselor, a social worker, a mom, a minister, a finance advisor, and more. In this position, I have the opportunity to impact the lives of young people just starting out. I help them get their grades up so they can go to college. I teach them job skills so they can pay their bills. I help them solve problems when they don't have friends or family to help. I can't imagine a more important job in this community."

That's from the manager of a fast-food restaurant: *I can't imagine a more important job in this community.* Do your front-line managers believe they have the most important job in their community?

Still, the question lingers. Can this type of heart-led leadership achieve bottom-line results even in fast-food restaurants? Is this all a pipe dream or is it cold, hard pragmatism? Well, the numbers don't lie.

The willingness of Popeyes franchisees to recommend the franchise is up 23 percent in Cheryl's tenure. The company has been growing for six years, with average restaurant sales up 25 percent. Market share has grown from 14 percent to 21 percent. Profitability is up 40 percent. Eighty percent of restaurants have been remodeled in the past two years. The stock is up 450 percent, outpacing both the S&P 500 restaurant sector and the total S&P 500. So much for the belief that this stuff is touchy-feely!

Cheryl says it is 100 percent about the metrics and about delivering superior performance results—but she is also on a mission to prove that these metrics are the result of heart-led leadership.

INCH #3: CARING

When you care for someone or something, whether a child, a client, an employee, or a potted plant, you want to see it do well. Too many leaders see caring for others as a sign of weakness. In reality, caring is all about strength. It takes strength to champion a purpose beyond profits, to step out of the spotlight, to support the vision of others, and to inspire them to find and follow a purpose. Cheryl Bachelder calls it "dignity." When strong leaders embrace human dignity and care enough about whom they lead, they truly make their people partners in the organization's pursuit of success.

4. Excuse Me, Sir, Is Something Wrong with Your Boots?

ALTHOUGH I GREW UP NOT FAR FROM NEW YORK CITY, I'VE COME TO love the West and the western way of life. I enjoy visiting working ranches, attending the barrel races at the National Western Stock Show, and rubbing shoulders with cowboys. For some reason, I feel at ease with cowhands and appreciate their values of hard work and humility. I sometimes joke with my wife that I must have been a cowboy in a previous life.

Of course, I live and work in a big city, Denver, and I usually wear a suit for work. But I like the fact that people in Denver sometimes wear cowboy boots with their suits. So I decided a couple of years ago that I needed a good pair of boots that I could wear around town. And if you ask anyone in the know in our area, they will tell you that Lucchese boots are the gold standard for quality cowboy boots handmade from exotic leathers.

Lucchese Bootmaker, founded in 1883, is head-quartered in El Paso, Texas, but the company has three flagship stores, in San Antonio, Santa Fe, and Nashville. I travel to Nashville frequently, and it's one of my favorite cities. I happened to be there not long ago for a meeting with a young executive I was coaching, and I decided the time was right to buy some Lucchese boots. Unfortunately, instead of going to the flagship Lucchese store, I wandered into a shop that sold boots in the tourist area on Broadway. I settled on a pair of boots and—without even measuring my feet—the salesman quickly told me that since the soft leather would stretch, I needed a size 8½ boot for my size 10 feet. I was a little surprised, but he was the expert, so I accepted his recommendation. "Son, this is soft ostrich leather and I guarantee it will stretch to fit your foot," he told me.

I was so excited to finally have a pair of Lucchese boots that I wore them out of the store and walked proudly to the Palm Restaurant, where I was having dinner with friends. All through dinner, though, my feet were killing me. Later in the evening, I walked back to the nearby Hilton Hotel, where I was staying. I sat in the lobby, took my boots off, and rubbed my sore feet. I was feeling depressed about the boots I'd bought. I was sitting there with a perplexed look on my face when, out of nowhere, a man walked up to me and said, "Excuse me, sir, is something wrong with your boots?"

I looked up and saw a man standing in front of me in pressed jeans, a cowboy hat, and a beautiful pair of

Lucchese alligator-skin boots. I didn't know who he was or where he had come from, but I told him the story of my purchase earlier that evening and how incredibly sore my feet were after wearing the boots for several hours.

"Do you mind if I take look?" he asked me.

"No, go ahead," I said.

He knelt in front of me, examined the boots, and felt my feet. Then he said, "Sir, these boots are too small for you." He also told me there was a small piece of leather inside the heel that needed more sanding. He suggested I try to return the boots to the store where I'd purchased them. "If the store won't take them back," he said, "send them to me and we'll accept a return."

With that, he handed me his card and walked away.

Still in shock from meeting this salesman savior who had come out of nowhere, I looked down at the business card he had given me. It read: *Jay Hamby, National Director of Retail Sales, Lucchese Bootmaker.*

I was floored by the coincidence of meeting a Lucchese executive and that he had offered to help a complete stranger with his boots late at night in the lobby of a Nashville hotel. That is exceptional customer service that goes above and beyond. It turned out that the store allowed me to return those boots. So when I got back home to Denver I sent Jay Hamby a handwritten thank-you note and a copy of my book to express my appreciation.

I didn't think about the incident again until some months later when I was in Santa Fe for a speech. My wife and I were staying at the Inn at Anasazi near Santa

Fe Plaza, and I noticed a Lucchese flagship store right on the square. So I decided to buy another pair of boots. The Lucchese saleswoman measured my feet and told me that I needed a size 9½. When I heard that, I told her the story of my earlier experience in Nashville with the size 8½ boots. Then she completely stunned me by asking, "Are you Tommy Spaulding?" I had to pick my jaw up off the floor. She explained that Jay Hamby had had all the Lucchese salespeople read my book and told them about his experience meeting me. Then she called Jay in his office and told him I was standing there in the Santa Fe store. Thanks to Jay, I walked out with two pairs of Lucchese boots and an even stronger sense of Lucchese's commitment to its customers.

I later called Jay and thanked him for encouraging Lucchese's sales staff to read my book. I learned that he had spent 18 years working for Ralph Lauren and firmly believed in what he calls the "luxury customer experience." I've talked to Jay any number of times over the years, and met him again when Lucchese asked me to speak at the company's annual meeting. His incredible passion and commitment to what he does have come through in every conversation I've ever had with him. Jay Hamby loves Lucchese boots—and he loves serving and helping the company's customers.

Jay Hamby's passion for boots reminds me a bit of my son Tate's passion for hockey. Tate is only seven years old, but he loves hockey so much that he wakes up four days a week at 5:00 a.m. so he can go practice. I can't tell you how many mornings I've dragged myself out of bed, bleary-eyed, to wake Tate up, only to see him hop up with a gleam in his eye and say, "It's a great day for hockey, Daddy!" It never ceases to amaze me. And when his team is finished with practice, Tate is always the last skater on the ice, staying until he gets kicked off by the Zamboni driver. The thing is, whether you're a seven-year-old boy who loves to play hockey or a man who loves to sell boots, it all comes down to the same thing—finding your passion.

Eventually Jay arranged for me to tour the Lucchese Bootmaker factory in El Paso with Sam Lucchese III, the great-great-grandson of the founder, Salvatore Lucchese. I learned that many of the Lucchese employees were the second or third generation in their families to work in the boot factory. I also discovered that more than 100 different sets of hands touch each pair of Lucchese boots before they make it to a retail shelf. It was a privilege to witness a culture that lives and breathes passion and pride, from the factory floor to the top of the organizational chart.

Whatever industry you are in, whatever your career, that type of passion and commitment and follow-through is an unparalleled asset, as well as a huge differentiation from your competitors and those around you. How many executives care deeply enough about what they do that they will sit down in a hotel lobby at 11:00 p.m. to help a stranger with his boots?

INCH #4: PASSION

The Greek word for *passion* means "to suffer." When something matters so much to you that you're willing to suffer to see it succeed, that's passion. It might come with pain and sacrifice, and it almost always comes with hard work, but it never comes without joy. Passion breeds commitment, enthusiasm, and effort—a willingness to go the extra mile for your organization, the people around you, and your customers. Whatever your job, title, or role, a passionate belief in what you do is often the difference between success and failure.

5. Death-to-Summit Ratio

MOUNT EVEREST IS THE HIGHEST AND PROBABLY THE MOST FA-
mous mountain in the world. There have been several thousand ascents of the 29,029-foot Himalayan peak
since Edmund Hillary first summited the mountain in
1953. But nearly 250 people have also lost their lives there.
In mountaineering terms, Everest has a death-to-summit
ratio of about 4 percent—for every 25 people who climb
Everest, one person dies in the attempt.

The world's second-highest mountain is K2, which
rises 28,251 feet high in the Karakoram Range. K2 is
known as the "savage mountain" because it's exceptionally
dangerous—it has a death-to-summit ratio of 40 percent.
There have been 375 summits of K2 and over 150 deaths.
For every 10 people who have climbed K2, four people
have died on the mountain.

Only nine Americans have stood on the summit of *both*
Everest and K2. One of them is my friend Chris Warner.

So I asked Chris what it takes to successfully conquer the two highest mountains in the world. Tenacity? Preparation? Willpower? Courage?

The answer obviously involves all of these traits to some degree, but Chris suggested the most important factor was something else altogether: selflessness.

"In mountaineering, if you put your own personal desires ahead of your team's goals," Chris said, "somebody is going to die."

Chris knows something about this, because in the course of leading 200 expeditions and summiting four of the world's six highest mountains, he has been in several precarious situations at high altitude. Here is his description of his successful summit of K2.

It was Chris's third attempt to climb this legendary mountain. His two previous efforts had failed, largely due to weather conditions and massive snowstorms. In 2007 he set out once more, joined by teammates Don Bowie of California and Bruce Normand of Scotland. On their second day after leaving base camp, Chris and Bruce nearly died while crossing a snow bridge. They were roped together when the snow collapsed and Bruce fell into a crevasse, pulling Chris with him.

"These crevasses are often hundreds of feet deep," said Chris. "They would never have found our bodies. I was being dragged across the snow toward the lip of this crevasse, knowing I was about to die, when suddenly the ground beneath me exploded and I fell into a separate crevasse."

By falling into different fissures, the two men became anchors for each other—dangling in the air by harnesses while their rope stretched across a section of snow that hadn't collapsed. As a result, they survived.

"It was a pure miracle," marveled Chris.

The team made several climbs up K2 in the next few weeks, first by themselves and then as part of a joint effort with climbers from other countries. After overcoming temperatures as low as 20 degrees below zero, winds that swirled up to 40 mph, and snow that was waist deep on parts of the climbing route, they finally reached Camp Four at 26,000 feet. Within sight of the peak, they made plans to leave in stages for their final ascent to the summit.

As Chris explained it, the first team goes out to break a trail and tie the rope for everyone else. The second team follows an hour later, catches the first team, and takes over responsibility for forging the path. In mountaineering, he said, "if I lead us to the first ledge, you lead us to the next."

The Korean team took the first legs, while Chris's team agreed to lead the middle stage. This was the most technically difficult section, as they needed to traverse a vertical ice face and climb a 55-degree slope in the shadow of a towering glacier that has been known to rain fatal chunks of ice onto climbers. A Russian team would take responsibility for the final stretch to the peak. They left camp in the middle of the night. When dawn broke the next day, the weather was gorgeous; everyone was thrilled to be climbing under a clear blue sky.

Then tragedy struck.

A Nepalese Sherpa who was with the Koreans (and who had previously summited Everest six times) slipped while unclipped from his rope. He tumbled down the slope and was launched off the mountain, falling 9,000 feet to his death, as the other climbers watched in horror.

"Everybody was completely gripped," Chris said. "The fear was so amazing that people could barely catch their breath. Here we were, watching someone die. And we knew, given the history of K2, there were likely to be more deaths. The odds were against us. Everybody was thinking, 'Am I next? Should I turn around or go on?'"

Chris went on. Partly, he said, it was that he felt strong and believed it was his time to finally conquer the peak. But he also reasoned that someone needed to climb up and assist the Korean team.

"They were understandably frozen in place," he said. "They needed someone to go up and free them from this fear, so they could at least descend if that's what they chose to do."

All of the well-laid plans of the night before were now out the window. The Koreans were in no condition to continue breaking the trail, and nobody knew if there was enough equipment left to reach the summit, since some rope and pitons were in the fallen Sherpa's backpack.

Chris, Don, and Bruce decided to split up. Don retreated to the end of the line and asked the trailing teams to send equipment to the lead climbers. Chris forged ahead and caught up to the Koreans. After helping them, he took the lead and climbed until he ran out of rope.

Then the Russian team made its way to the front with the remaining rope and took the lead. The spontaneous plan cobbled together by the climbers worked. By sharing the load and responsibility and by doing what was best for the group at each moment, they succeeded in reaching the summit. When they radioed down to announce their success, applause broke out from tent to tent across base camp.

It was a triumphant moment near the top of the world. The view atop those peaks is breathtaking, Chris says. He recalled an earlier time when he had summited Everest and sat by himself for a few moments.

"I could see the curvature of the Earth," he said. "It was late morning and the sky above me was violet, but I could still see stars twinkling. I had the feeling that, instead of being at the top of the world, I was actually at the bottom of space."

This time on K2, though, it wasn't late morning. Because of the complications during the ascent, it was now late afternoon and the climbers knew they'd be descending into a gathering darkness. On the way down, Bruce, Chris, and Don passed two Italian climbers, Marco and Stefano, who were still trying to summit. Then, at 8:00 p.m., they found a Czech climber, Libor, collapsed in the snow. He was conscious but unable to walk, so they hoisted him up and dragged him back to camp in the darkness.

In the morning, the climbers awoke to a blizzard, which meant they urgently needed to get down to the safety of Camp Three. They also learned that Marco, one of the last two Italians on the mountain, had returned to camp about midnight, but without his teammate. Stefano was doubtless dead by this point, having likely frozen to death in the menacing subzero cold of the previous night. Then, as the climbers descended that day through the storm, Don slipped and crashed down the slope. He survived but suffered a broken leg. Chris accompanied the still sick Czech climber down the mountain. They all eventually made it to base camp—Don with the help of other climbers who'd hiked up the mountain with a makeshift stretcher.

"It felt as if we were coming down K2 with everything falling apart around us," Chris said. "I was the last person on that expedition down the mountain, and I was checking every tent I came across. I didn't want to leave anyone else behind to die."

Chris remembers the climb as one of the most intense experiences of his life. But he uses lessons from these expeditions in other ventures. He has, for instance, led groups of inexperienced climbers up Mount Kilimanjaro in Tanzania, using the same credos of selflessness and teamwork.

"The only way to achieve this goal," he tells them, "is to fall in love with other people in the group. You have to create an emotional bond with people on your team, because the time will come on the mountain when you need to find something inside yourself to give to another person."

He takes the same approach to entrepreneurial ventures. Aside from being an author, speaker, and teacher at the Wharton School of Business, Chris is the CEO of Earth

Treks, which operates indoor climbing centers, a rock- and ice-climbing school, and a mountaineering guide service. When he founded the business, he modeled it on a climbing partnership, one of mutual dependence among team members.

"Whether you're on the mountain or at your job, the question is, how do you avoid failure? Most people die on mountains because of human error," he said. "Often the most dangerous thing we face is the people we're climbing with. So I try to pick partners who have the behavioral traits that suggest they'll work well together. I do the same thing with my business."

He strives to hire people who share similar values and are willing to give their all to the organization's success, just as if they were climbing a mountain together and leading each other from ledge to ledge. In return, employees are treated as partners in the business, even splitting a share of the profits.

His words reminded me of an idea that has been on my mind for many years. I call it the "I/we ratio." The premise is simple. Whenever I listen to a leader speaking, I take out a small notebook and put checkmarks on a page when I hear the word *I* or *we*. I've found it to be an incredible predictor of whether someone is a servant leader or a self-serving leader.

The worst ratio I ever came across was at a Denver Rotary Club meeting with a now retired Colorado politician. He used the word *I* a total of 67 times, and *we* only three times. Needless to say, he was not a heart-led leader. I'm certain that Chris and other successful climbers would easily pass the "I/we ratio" test.

In the end, Chris told me, in both mountaineering and business, you can't let your personal desires conflict with the team's goals. So whether your test is the "I/we ratio" or the death-to-summit ratio, the solution is always the same: success stems from teamwork, and teamwork is driven by selflessness.

INCH #5: SELFLESSNESS

"In mountaineering, if you put your own personal desires ahead of your team's goals," Chris Warner says, "somebody is going to die." Of course, how we engage with our people on a daily basis isn't a life-and-death situation like climbing K2, but the same rules apply. Heart-led leaders understand that success results from collaboration and shared responsibility. Self-serving leaders value personal goals and agendas over the needs of the team. Heart-led leaders think in the "we," while self-serving leaders are all about the "me."

6. Drawing Straws

———

THE FIRST TIME I MET BILL GRAEBEL, HE PUT ME IN A GOLF CART AND gave me a tour of his 300,000-square-foot warehouse. That building, out by Denver International Airport, is one of the largest storage facilities on the planet. It serves as the epicenter for Graebel Companies, the world's largest privately held relocation firm. As we drove through a seemingly endless maze of aisles and corridors, I saw movers, truckers, forklift operators, and other employees engaged in the hard labor that goes into coordinating the 60,000 moves that Graebel manages annually in 120 countries. I was impressed by the vast size of the operation. But what really struck a chord with me was the fact that Bill knew just about every employee's name.

In all my years, I've never seen a CEO of a company that size who knew the names of every employee. Whether someone is white-collar or blue-collar, at the top of the org chart or at the bottom, doesn't matter to Bill. He not only knew the names of every employee but also knew something special about most of them.

That golf cart ride took place 15 years ago, when I was director of corporate relations at Up with People and Bill was president of Graebel Movers. Today Bill is the CEO of Graebel Companies. The firm was founded by his father in 1950 and now encompasses six divisions and 2,400 employees. He oversees a large international operation, and yet his style of management hasn't changed a bit. Even as CEO, he tries to meet regularly with as many employees as possible, regardless of their position or title within the company. He walks the halls of his world headquarters like an athlete on a treadmill. And every time I visit Bill in his office, he takes the elevator down three flights to greet me in the lobby. Do you greet your customers and clients at the front door of your building or at your office door? There is a difference—and your customers and clients know it.

I have spoken to Graebel's worldwide staff, customers, and global partners a half dozen times, including in Prague, Czech Republic. And regardless of the location, I've discovered that Graebel's culture is special. It emanates from the top and epitomizes the midwestern values of Bill's hometown, Wausau, Wisconsin—values like honesty, humility, and a strong work ethic. Every time I talk with Bill's employees or customers, they invariably use the same words to describe him. "Bill is the most genuine man I have ever met," they tell me. When you hear the same words over and over again, it's not a coincidence.

I went over to Bill's office one day recently for a meeting. (Naturally, he met me in the lobby.) We talked for a while about my National Leadership Academy, which is formally called the Ben Graebel National Leadership Academy after Bill's older brother. The two brothers were best friends and, with their father, managed Graebel Companies together. Tragically, Ben died of a heart attack five years ago. I named the academy in Ben's honor because the Graebels have always been tremendous supporters of my efforts to instill the values of servant leadership in young people. After discussing plans for that year's Academy, I reminisced with Bill about my first encounter with him 15 years earlier and how I had admired the personal connection he made with so many employees.

Bill told me of a recent trip he'd made to Singapore, where Graebel Companies had opened an office. Bill told his staff that he wanted a chance to meet the new Singaporean employees one-on-one.

"Obviously, it's very unusual in the Asian culture for employees to meet individually with their bosses like that, and some of them were hesitant to sign up for a meeting time," he said. "But one of the other international staff members there explained to everyone why I was interested in getting to know our staff. So we eventually found a time for each person to meet with me.

"I'll never forget this one meeting, with a woman who had a very quiet, reserved personality. And she kept saying to me, over and over again, 'I'm so honored to meet with you.' I just wanted to laugh because, honestly, Tommy, I do this because I'm interested in people. I like getting to know them. And not only that, but our company is so much better off when our people feel valued."

Bill feels it's important for leaders not only to maintain a connection to their staff and employees but also to involve as many people as possible in conversations about the business. "Nobody knows all the answers, so why not just admit up front that we don't know every answer?" he said. "When employees these days see managers or co-workers who act like they know it all, it comes across to them as lacking in integrity."

Given Graebel's expansion abroad, I asked Bill whether this management style of valuing every individual translated to other cultures.

"Well, that's a good question. Because a big worry of ours is whether this 'secret sauce,' so to speak, of Graebel culture does transfer to other countries. I think you find that there is always respect for one's title or position, but that could just be organizational respect. That's not enough for us. At Graebel, we want people to respect the person they report to and not just the position."

RESPECT THE PERSON, NOT the position. I think that's an ideal that all Who Leaders should strive for. People are hungry for heart-led leaders who are genuine, and they aren't fooled by disingenuousness. But what does a truly authentic leader look like? Well, Bill Graebel is certainly one example to emulate. And I believe my friend Tim Stojka in Chicago is another.

Tim is a technology entrepreneur and the co-founder and CEO of Agentis Energy, which provides software to utility companies. I first met Tim at a Young Presidents' Organization leadership conference and was instantly drawn to him. Jill and I quickly became fast friends with Tim and his beautiful wife, Effie. To me, Tim has always come across as a genuine and humble individual. And a few years ago I discovered he is like that with every person he meets.

I happened to be in Chicago for work, so Tim arranged to take me to a White Sox baseball game and then put me up at his home in suburban Chicago. There I met his three children and Effie's mother, YiaYia, who lives with them. It was a pleasure to watch Tim with his children and to feel the love, support, and nurturing care that he, his wife, and his mother-in-law provide. The next morning, after a wonderful Greek breakfast, I joined Tim and his son, John, for a golf outing at Butler National Golf Club outside of Chicago.

Out on the course, we were introduced to our young caddy, Connor. A senior in high school, Connor was at the time applying to be an Evans Scholar at the University of Illinois. He was as polite as any caddy I've ever met. I remember thinking that he was the kind of young man I want my daughter to marry one day.

A few holes into the round, I found myself alone with

Connor. He asked me how long I had known Mr. Stojka. "A few years," I said, "but we've actually gotten pretty close in that time."

I asked Connor if he had ever caddied for Tim before. "No, I'm usually not that lucky," he replied.

I thought that was an unusual answer. "What do you mean?" I asked him.

Connor told me that whenever Tim golfed at Butler, the other caddies would fight for the opportunity to caddy for him. Usually they resorted to drawing straws. "And today," Connor said with a proud smile, "I drew the longest straw."

"He must be a great tipper," I joked.

And then Connor said something that made me respect Tim even more.

"I don't know if Mr. Stojka is a good tipper," he told me candidly, "but I do know that he is the nicest and most genuine of all our members."

I was impressed. Tim had developed a reputation for being so authentic and down to earth that others actually drew straws to hang out with him. And so for the rest of that round, I couldn't help asking myself: Is anyone drawing straws to hang out with me?

INCH #6: AUTHENTICITY

Respect begins with authenticity. When people respect a leader—the person, not the position—they enthusiastically follow—at home, at work, in your community, even on the golf course!

7. Twisted Who

———

J AY JAY FRENCH HAS PERFORMED ONSTAGE, WHILE DRESSED IN DRAG, in front of tens of thousands of screaming fans. He is the founder and lead guitarist of Twisted Sister, whose "We're Not Gonna Take It" is one of the most celebrated rock anthems of all time. By any definition, Jay Jay French is a rock star.

But if you met him offstage, you probably wouldn't peg him as a celebrity. Although Jay Jay is grateful for his musical success, he seems more at home as an entrepreneur and a doting father. He is a rock star who abstains from both drugs and alcohol. And he is more comfortable in his own skin than almost anyone else I know.

I first met Jay Jay at an Extreme Leadership Summit conference in San Diego. I was expecting to meet a stereotypical rock star, pretentious and self-absorbed, when I greeted him offstage, but Jay Jay was down to earth and genuine. We hit it off, so the next time I was in New York I called Jay Jay (or John, as I've come to know him). We went for a walk in Central Park and talked about business and life. I asked him how he is able to be so confident—anyone who spends his time dressing in drag onstage has to be self-assured!

"When I was a teenager, I sold drugs in my neighborhood. It made me popular and helped me see that I had good business skills. Then I was involved in the antiwar movement of the 1960s and became pretty well known for that. So the more successful and popular I became, the more confident I became. Now, I obviously don't recommend that people deal drugs—I am very anti-drugs today—but the point is to find something you're good at, because success breeds confidence. And confidence breeds success."

Jay Jay was self-aware enough to realize early on that drugs would tear his life apart. So he stopped doing drugs and alcohol cold turkey and never looked back. "I could see the drug scene was going to destroy me. So I asked myself, 'Where is this going? Are you going to get arrested? Die from an overdose? Get murdered during a drug deal?' I made the decision that enough was enough," he told me. "By the time I formed Twisted Sister, I was so far past that part of my life when I dealt drugs. I became so anti-drugs that I fired people [from the band] for drug use. I hate what drugs do to people. It keeps them from achieving their potential."

Jay Jay first formed Twisted Sister in 1972, when he was in his early twenties, but it took 10 years for the group to land a record contract. Jay Jay was the lead guitarist and manager. "I think I'm a businessman who happens to play guitar," he says now, rather than a rock star who happens to manage the band. Twisted Sister achieved its greatest fame with its third album, which came out in 1984. The band broke up four years later when the members couldn't stand being around one another anymore. Jay Jay's professional and personal life crashed at the same time, as his marriage broke up and he declared bankruptcy. Although he remarried a few years later and became a father, he spent several years struggling to rebuild his musical career.

"Then one day my wife said to me, 'You know, you've had success, you've had your day in the sun, maybe it's time to do something else.' So I got a job selling stereos. I'd go to residences on the East Side of Manhattan to measure and install equipment. I was hired help—I often had to use the servants' entrance. In some apartments, I'd see Twisted Sister albums on the shelves. But I never said anything. I was trying to move on with my life."

It's a steep drop from rock star to stereo salesman. I asked Jay Jay if his fall from fame humbled him.

"Actually, I never felt like I succumbed to stardom to begin with, so I wasn't crushed by it," he said. "Nobody *owns* stardom. The public allows you to rent it, and every celebrity has a window that will eventually close. I never believed it would last forever. When everything fell apart in 1988–89, I knew it would take time to put the pieces of my life back together. But I also knew I'd get through it because the trauma didn't compare to what I experienced when I was 22 years old. At the time, I was in love with a beautiful girl and I was in the first version of Twisted Sister. Then—all in the same week—my mother died, my girl-friend left me, and the band broke up. That week almost crushed me. I was depressed for months. But it proved to me I could survive anything."

Jay Jay rebooted his life by forming a management company and becoming a successful producer. And then, after reuniting for a 9/11 fund-raiser, Twisted Sister started performing again in 2003; today the band tours regularly worldwide. Jay Jay is back in his role as manager-guitarist. But instead of resting on his laurels, he is launching a new career as a motivational speaker and author.

"I like to talk to people about how I got through chal-lenges in my life and how they can do so, too," he said. "Look, 99 percent of people are just trying to get through their day. Sometimes you just want to put a sheet over your head, but I tell them that successful people don't shy away from confronting difficult situations. You need to be truth-ful with yourself. Boldly truthful. Crisis doesn't build char-acter; crisis exposes character."

What impressed me most about Jay Jay is that through all the stages of his life—from teenage rebel to rock star to stereo salesman to producer to resurrected rock star to motivational speaker—he retained a remarkable level of self-awareness. This awareness convinced him to quit drugs cold turkey when he was 20 years old, kept him from suc-cumbing to the temptations of stardom, and helped him survive what could have been an emotionally devastating fall from grace. He always seemed to know who he was and what was important to him.

When I raised that with him, he told me a story about some friends of his. "They were teenagers at the time and they snuck into the Dakota when John Lennon was still alive, and they met him and spent an hour with him, just talking. One of them told Lennon that he didn't know what he wanted to do with his life. And do you know what Lennon said to him? He said, 'You're asking the wrong question. It's not *what* are you going to do, it's *who* are you going to be. That's the question.' Well, that *is* the question, isn't it? And I suppose once you figure that out, then it helps you get through everything else you're going to confront in life."

INCH #7: SELF-AWARENESS

John Lennon said it best: "It's not *what* you are going to do, it's *who* are you going to be." Heart-led leaders have the self-awareness to understand who they are and what's important to them. They can step outside of themselves, giving themselves the ability not just to see their own strengths and weaknesses but also to make decisions about how best to live their lives and serve those around them.

8. Am I Going to Die?

——

NINE-YEAR-OLD BOYS ARE CURIOUS AND ADVENTUROUS BY NATURE. As any parent of young boys knows, their quest for excitement often results in scraped knees and occasionally some stitches or a broken bone. A little innocent mischief, however, isn't supposed to take a nine-year-old boy to within inches of death and forever alter his life.

When John O'Leary was nine, he saw some boys in the neighborhood perform a fun trick and decided to try it for himself. The boys would pour gasoline on the sidewalk, then step back and throw a match. The liquid would ignite and dance around enchantingly for a few seconds.

"It looked awesome," John remembers. And it seemed harmless to him.

So one weekend day when his parents were busy, John went to the garage, lit a piece of cardboard on fire, and put it on the floor. He opened a can of gasoline and tipped it gently toward the flames, expecting to see fiery sparks leap into the air when gasoline dripped onto the burning cardboard. But before any liquid escaped from the can, the gasoline vapors wafting out of the container sucked the fire back into it.

And John's world burst into flames.

The container exploded with such force that John was thrown into the air, against the side of the garage. When he stood up, he was on fire. He ran screaming through the flames and into his house.

His 17-year-old brother grabbed a rug and beat down the fire, ignoring the searing heat and flames that threatened to overwhelm them both. For more than two minutes, he swung that rug until he extinguished the fire.

"What he did was nothing short of miraculous," John said. "He saved my life."

John was rushed to the hospital. There were burns on 100 percent of his body.

Most of us know the pain of accidentally touching a hot stove or pan. Our skin turns red and it hurts more than we could have imagined. Those are first-degree burns. A second-degree burn is one that burns through the first layer of skin and results in agonizing blisters. And a third-degree burn is one that singes every layer of skin, burning through nerves and sometimes into muscle or bone. The result is flesh that turns black and charred, or white and leathery.

John O'Leary had third-degree burns on 87 percent of his body, and second-degree burns everywhere else.

His chance of survival was near zero. Doctors and nurses thought he would die before morning.

Today, three decades later, my friend John O'Leary is a successful motivational speaker, an entrepreneur, and president of Rising Above, a leadership lifestyle organization designed to encourage people to lead inspired lives. He has a beautiful wife and four lovely children. He has survived and thrived. And he has done so through the power of what he calls faithfulness.

"Part of it for me is faith in a higher power, but it doesn't have to mean that for everyone," he told me. "Determination and grit are part of faithfulness. To me, faithfulness means having the faith and the belief to keep taking that next step, to keep putting one foot in front of the other."

Taking it one step at a time is what brought John to where he is today. His journey was not an easy one.

That first day, as John lay in his hospital bed, he was in agony. His eyes were swollen shut. His lungs were burned, making it excruciating to take a breath. I've seen pictures of John in that hospital bed, and they are shocking: an innocent little boy whose entire body has been scorched by flames. It is a scene that is almost beyond words.

His mom sat down next to his bed that night and told him that she loved him.

"Mom, am I going to die?" John asked her.

"Have you ever asked a question where you didn't want to know the answer?" John says now. "I wanted my mom to tell me that we were going to get a milkshake that night.

That's what I wanted to hear. But she gave me the truth in the form of a question, and it took a lot of audacity and love."

"Baby, do you want to die?" she asked her son. "Because it's your choice, not mine."

"It took courage and boldness," John says. "But she made me walk over to the cliff with her. She pointed down and said, 'That's one way you can go. But you can choose this other way instead.'"

"I don't want to die, Mom," John answered. "I want to live."

"Good," she said. "Then take the hand of God, walk the journey with him, and baby, you fight like you've never fought before."

John spent five months in the hospital fighting for life. Without skin, the possibility of acquiring a fatal infection is enormously high, and death is considered not just possible but likely.

"But after that first night, the question of survival was never one we considered. Not once after that did I consider death as an option," he said. He just kept putting one foot in front of the other.

While in the hospital, John withstood 24 surgeries, numerous skin grafts, and the amputations of all of his fingers (the surgeons cut into his palms and utilized the bones above his knuckles to form tiny, nub-like fingers that John uses to this day). He endured a tracheotomy, which helped him breathe but rendered him unable to eat, drink, or talk. He tolerated daily blood draws from his toes, medication that made him vomit, and endless hours of anguishing physical and occupational therapy. But one of his most painful memories is of undergoing the daily two-hour process of changing his bandages.

"It was an arduous process, and the pain was indescribable," he said. "You know what it's like to burn yourself on a hot stove. Well, imagine that pain multiplied across your entire body. Every day the nurses took the bandages off my body, where there was no skin, then put more medication on before wrapping me in new bandages.

"I just wanted to go home with my mom and dad," John said. "For most of the time I was in the hospital, I couldn't be touched. I was a nine-year-old boy who just wanted to lie down with my parents again and feel them next to me."

When John did finally go home, he was in a wheelchair and couldn't walk. He had no fingers and couldn't hold anything in his hands. His body was scarred and broken. But he was alive. He had a future.

His survival was considered a miracle. His family stayed in touch with the nurses who had cared for him, loved him, and nurtured him back to life. Many of them attended his wedding two decades later. But one nurse drifted out of touch, an African American man named Roy who played an important role in John's recovery.

"Every day Nurse Roy would come get me for therapy," John recalled. "I could barely move my legs and didn't believe I'd ever walk again. A lot of people didn't think I'd walk. But he'd pick me up and half carry me down the hall. And he would whisper in my ear, 'Boy, you will walk again. And I'm going to walk with you.'"

John always wondered what happened to Nurse Roy. He wished he could say thank you to the man who showed faith in him. Then, a few years ago, John was speaking at a conference and one of the hosts, who knew his story, asked him about Nurse Roy. John recounted the tale for the audience.

"Then I heard a microphone click on and I heard this voice say, 'Boy, you are walking again! And I am proud to walk with you!' The curtain pulled back and out walked Nurse Roy. I couldn't believe it. The sponsors had hired a private investigator to find him. We had an incredible time together that night."

Roy told him he was amazed at John's survival and his success. "But what surprises me the most," he said, "is to learn, after 27 years, that my work and my life mattered."

"Can you imagine? Roy never knew the full degree to which his life mattered," John whispered.

"I know there are days for all of us," John went on, "when we go home and put our head on the pillow and say, 'Is it worth it? Isn't there an easier way?' Well, heck yes, it's worth it! It's worth it every day!"

John credits the love he felt from everyone around him—his parents, siblings, doctors, and nurses—with helping him to endure and to grow into the person he has become.

"There are two things that motivate us in life. Fear and love. When you feel such powerful love from those around you, you finally start believing in yourself. When love shows up in our life, it changes us. And when we show up as love for those around us, we change them.

"Whatever we choose to focus on will grow around us. If you focus on the negativity, watch out, because it's coming. But if you focus on the possibility and the beauty of tomorrow, well, watch out, because that is coming, too!"

John still has nubs for fingers. But he has learned how to drive a car, type on his smartphone, even play the piano. His body still has scars that draw glances from people on the street, and he still has pain every day. But he has become an inspiration to everyone who meets him.

A couple of years ago John was visiting Denver for an event with the Colorado Rockies, and our families watched a ballgame together at Coors Field. When my then five-year-old son Tate met John, he asked him innocently, "Where are your fingers?"

"Little man, fingers are overrated!" John exclaimed, and then gave Tate a high five.

The response was typical of how John approaches every day of his life. I asked him how he persevered, how he turned his pain and scars into such a positive outlook.

"It comes back to faithfulness," he said. "We all make excuses as to why we can't do something. But we need to find a way to live up to the fullness of our potential. It doesn't matter who you are. We have to quit making excuses. Everyone has burns in life. Maybe they're not physical burns like mine are, but a lot of people walk around with emotional burns they need to overcome.

"When I was nine, I was happy and healthy, I had parents who loved me, I lived in a great community. Then everything blew up. Well, sometimes life blows up. And then what? Faithfulness is the belief that you can take that next step forward. It means loving life and choosing to thrive and taking on life in the best way you can every single day."

INCH #8: FAITHFULNESS

Whether you're an entrepreneur launching a new business, an individual starting over after the loss of a job, a student just trying to finish school, or someone overcoming a life-changing circumstance, the question is the same: do you have the belief it takes to keep putting one foot in front of the other? Heart-led leaders fulfill their potential one faithful step at a time.

9. When No One Else Is Looking

———

ONE OF THE EARLIEST WHO LEADER LESSONS I LEARNED TOOK place when I was a teenager participating in a Boy Scout camp. At the time, I wasn't content to be just a regular Scout. I wanted to excel. So I pushed myself to earn the rank of Eagle Scout, the most elite of the elite in the Boy Scouts—only a very small percentage of the boys who join the Boy Scouts reach that rank. I became the youngest Eagle Scout in the history of my troop in Suffern, New York. Later, when I attended a Scouting camp one summer during high school, I made it my goal to be named Outstanding Scout, an honor our scoutmasters told us would be awarded to the individual who best demonstrated leadership and character.

I wanted so badly to win that award I could taste it. For the next couple of weeks I worked as hard as I could. I kept my tent and campsite immaculate. I hustled everywhere, and when the camp leaders were looking I hustled even more. I strived to be a leader around other Scouts. By the time camp was finished, I was certain that no one had out-worked me, outhustled me, or shown more leadership than me. So when all of the campers and troop leaders gathered on the last night in front of a roaring campfire under a sky full of stars, I felt certain they were going to call my name as the winner of that summer's Outstanding Scout award.

When the time came, the scoutmaster made a speech about the importance of leadership and character. "And in our judgment, the Scout who has best demonstrated those traits this summer is . . ." I took a deep breath and started to stand up. ". . . Greg Brown."

Greg Brown? What? I was stunned. Greg Brown wasn't a better Scout than I was. He wasn't a better leader than I was. He hadn't outworked me during camp. How could they not have noticed all of my efforts, my skills, my expe-rience, and my leadership qualities? Greg Brown? Were they kidding? I went to bed that night utterly confused and frustrated.

The next morning, when camp was over and we were waiting around for our parents to come pick us up, I hap-pened to find myself standing next to the scoutmaster. So I managed, a bit awkwardly, to steer the conversation toward the Outstanding Scout presentation. "Tell me about Greg Brown," I said. "Why did he win the award?"

The scoutmaster looked at me and put his hand on my shoulder. "Tommy boy," he said, "you're a great Scout and I know that you may have worked harder than any other young man here this summer."

I nodded.

"But leadership is about more than hard work," he said. "Leadership is also about character."

He then told me a story about something that had happened a week earlier, unbeknownst to me or any of the other Scouts. "We put a large fallen tree branch on the path between your campsite and the cafeteria," he told me. "And then we hid in the woods to see what would happen when you all encountered that obstacle on the path. We watched as you and a hundred other Scouts walked down that path and, one by one, stepped over that tree branch on your way to grab a cheeseburger at the cafeteria. Greg Brown was late to lunch that day. Because when he noticed the branch there, he stayed behind and worked all by himself to move that branch off the path."

The scoutmaster reminded me that leadership was about character. He said, looking me straight in the eye, "Character is what you do when no one else is looking."

CHARACTER IS WHAT YOU *do when no one else is looking.* That lesson made a great impression on me; I've never forgotten it. I learned that character means doing the right thing at all times, regardless of whether someone else is looking. Even if this means that you sometimes need to shovel some manure.

David Craig is currently the general manager of the C Lazy U Ranch a few hours outside of Denver. The C Lazy U is a high-end dude ranch that offers an enormous array

of activities on its 8,500-acre spread in the Rocky Mountains, from fly fishing and mountain biking in the summer
to cross-country skiing and snowmobiling in the winter.
But the ranch is especially known for its horseback riding
program. Since my daughter happens to love horseback
riding, we decided not long ago to take a family vacation
at the C Lazy U. That is when I learned about David's penchant for getting down in the trenches with his staff and
doing whatever is necessary to keep his operation running
smoothly, no matter what the task or who is watching.

The ranch has a herd of more than 180 horses, and
each guest is matched with a horse that fits that person's
riding ability. You can take your horse out twice daily with
wranglers who guide outings on nearby mountain trails.
When ranch guests line up outside for the morning ride,
the staff call out names and lead people to their horses.
With more than 180 horses on the ranch, however, these
animals produce quite a bit of manure every day.

On our first day at the ranch, as the staff matched
guests with their horses, I saw David walking around with
a manure rake, picking up the horse droppings. I thought
it was wonderful that he was willing to take on one of the
most thankless jobs to show that even the general manager was concerned about keeping the ranch clean and
the guests happy. I was more surprised when I saw him out
there on the second day. And I was shocked to see him
doing the same thing on the third day, the fourth, and the
fifth. In fact, David picked up manure every single morning of our weeklong stay at the C Lazy U.

It was such a surprise to see the general manager undertaking the most menial of tasks that all of the guests began talking about it among ourselves. I heard many comments along the lines of "That general manager has shoveled more sh*t all week than any of his employees. I wish my executives and managers worked that hard."

David certainly exhibited attention to detail and a concern for putting the customer first—but he was also setting an example for his staff. After all, if the boss is willing to do the dirty work, then how could staff members see such a task as beneath them? David showed that he was concerned above all with doing the right thing. It reminded me of the example that Greg Brown had set many years ago at our Boy Scout camp—doing the right thing regardless of whether someone else was looking.

I RECENTLY CAME ACROSS another example of this in a corporate environment when I did some work with Stream Global Services. Stream (which has since merged with Convergys) is a business process outsourcing (BPO) company with 37,000 employees in 22 countries. In preparation for a speaking engagement addressing Stream's worldwide team, I made arrangements to visit three call centers in Arizona and El Salvador and to facilitate a one-hour team-building exercise with the company's senior managers.

During the team-building meeting, I was introduced to the chief operating officer, Brian Delaney. I was impressed with the entire team, but especially with Brian, who had been a public school teacher in the Bronx before embarking on a business career. Hardworking, intense, and passionate about his job, Brian was also genuine and gentle. He asked me what it was like to be on the speaking circuit full-time, and I told him the truth—that I love what I do, but it gets lonely on the road, and I miss my family terribly.

A month later, I headed to Central America to spend a couple of days at one of Stream's call centers in San Salvador. It was the week before Christmas. While I was there, my assistant in Denver informed me that a major snowstorm was moving through the front range of the Rockies and that Denver International Airport might have to shut down. I was concerned about having my flight canceled on the way home and missing Christmas with my family.

My flight back home took me through Dallas. When I landed there for a layover, still wondering if the weather was going to wreak havoc on my connecting flight to Denver, I saw this email from Brian Delaney on my phone:

> *Tommy,*
> *Just as a backup escape route for you . . . I had my admin,*
> *Suzanne, reserve you a seat on a United flight that leaves*
> *Dallas at 4:47 p.m. today. We did not change anything on*
> *your original itinerary; I just wanted something in place for*
> *you if weather here in Denver causes your American connection*
> *to be canceled. Please call me or Suzanne if the American flight*
> *is canceled and we will ticket the United flight for you.*
> *Take care,*
> *Brian*

That American Airlines flight was indeed canceled. But thanks to Brian, I made the last United flight back to Denver before the airport closed down due to the storm. I was beyond grateful. I was also somewhat astounded—the chief operating officer of a company with 37,000 employees was concerned enough about me, an outside consultant, getting home to my family that he made time in his busy schedule to do something about it.

I shared this story when I spoke to Stream's worldwide team. I told them that, to me, this gesture defined the culture of their company, a place where the little things drive the big things. I have spoken to hundreds of organizations over the years, and many of them have done big things to show their appreciation. But none of those big gestures has ever meant more than Brian Delaney's small act of kindness. In the end, it doesn't matter if what you do is a little thing or a big thing—it's about doing the *right* thing.

INCH #9: CHARACTER

Character is what you do when no one is looking. It's a fundamental trait of heart-led leaders. They strive to do the right thing regardless of what others think or see. The famous "Cadet Prayer" that students at West Point learn includes a line summing this up perfectly: "Make us to choose the harder right instead of the easier wrong, and never to be content with a half-truth when the whole can be won." When you choose the harder right over the easier wrong—even when no one is looking—you are truly leading with your heart.

10. Everyone Has a Story

———

WHEN JODI ROLLAND WAS IN THE FIRST GRADE, SOMEONE ASKED her what she wanted to be when she grew up. She answered that she wanted to "work in a skyscraper and have an office with big windows." Four decades later, Jodi works in a tall office building and, from her corner office, she can gaze out large windows at the skyline of Denver while she tackles her dual roles as president of Bank of America, Colorado, and managing director for Merrill Lynch U.S. Wealth Management. From this perspective, it might seem as if Jodi was always destined for success. But her rise in the corporate world was anything but inevitable. In fact, she had to overcome a difficult childhood and numerous personal challenges. A few years ago she was reluctant to share her story with others. Now she sees it as a vital part of who she is and what she wants to accomplish.

I've known Jodi for several years. She reached out to me after reading my first book and through a mutual friend asked if we could meet. So we had coffee together and almost instantly became friends. I later asked Jodi to speak to our National Leadership Academy high school students about her journey to becoming one of the most high-ranking women in the financial industry. The students were enthralled by her story; it showed them not only that persistence and heart can overcome obstacles but also that a willingness to be vulnerable and open with others and to talk about the pain and adversity you've gone through can be a sign of strength.

Jodi grew up in a small town in Minnesota called Thief River Falls, about 70 miles from Canada, with a population of fewer than 10,000 people. Her family was at the low end of the middle class. When Jodi was seven, her mom died unexpectedly from a heart attack in her sleep—and Jodi was sleeping in the same bed with her when it happened. Her father was an alcoholic; her mom had been the glue that kept the family together. The rest of her childhood was a difficult one, growing up without a mother and with a father who drank a lot and who struggled financially.

After high school, Jodi worked days and took community college classes at night. When she was 19 years old she received a company bonus of $5,000. She decided to invest the money after receiving a cold call from a financial advisor. But the investment turned out to be a scam, and she lost every dollar. Nonetheless, she considers the loss of the money a fortuitous moment in her life.

"Believe it or not, that was the spark for me wanting to learn about financial management. I figured there had to be honest financial advisors out there, and I decided then that I wanted to become one," she said.

So Jodi began working toward a business degree from the University of North Dakota, which was located two and a half hours from her home. For the next three years she commuted five hours round-trip to her classes and returned home to work the night shift as a waitress at the American Legion. She went through five cars in three years—"and hit three deer and one moose along the way," she laughs. After graduating, she moved to Minneapolis to look for a job in the financial services industry.

"At that time, the business was even more male-dominated than it is today," she recalled. "I wanted to work as a financial advisor, but one executive who interviewed me only wanted to hire me as an assistant. I said no. Through sheer persistence, though, I finally got hired at Merrill Lynch."

Jodi's skill at building relationships—and her relentless work ethic—brought her considerable success as a financial advisor. Six years later she accepted a position in management, and she and her husband left Minneapolis for Denver. They also started a family. After having a son, they ran into difficulty having a second child; over the next five years, Jodi had eight miscarriages. Yes, eight. But she was determined that her son not be an only child. So she and her husband put each miscarriage behind them and kept trying.

All the while, Jodi continued to climb the corporate ladder. In 2009 she was named Western Division manager and director for Merrill Lynch, responsible for one-third of the United States, working out of corporate headquarters in New York. But when she became pregnant once again, Jodi decided to commute to the East Coast for work rather than change doctors. Then, two months after accepting her new position, she was prescribed bed rest and had to stop working.

She eventually gave birth to a baby boy. Born prematurely, he required special care for several months. Her family's personal challenges coincided with the fallout from the worst financial crisis since the Great Depression. Jodi was dealing with a perfect storm of demands on her time, and she and her employer realized that she needed to take a step back. So she agreed to move to a position within the company with fewer responsibilities.

"I've never been a person who said, 'Poor me.' If you go back to my childhood, to college, to my early career, and to my determination to have children, I just keep pushing forward," Jodi told me. "So I accepted a demotion, took some sideways jobs, and then moved back up." In 2011 she became managing director for Merrill Lynch's Heartland Market. In 2013 she added the title of president for Bank of America, Colorado.

In her speech, Jodi had two messages to give the students at the National Leadership Academy. One was that people are defined by "how they respond to adverse circumstances." The other was that it's OK to be open, candid, and vulnerable with others. "I had always felt that you need to appear confident even if you're not," she said.

"And, being a woman in a male-dominated field, I didn't want to risk being seen as an emotional leader"—a leader who is ruled by his or her emotions.

Jodi told me that she had only started opening up more to others recently, when she began looking for ways to build greater trust with her leadership team, clients, and customers. She realized that a shift toward openness, candor, and vulnerability might help. Jodi started talking more about herself with colleagues; she even gave a talk in which she discussed some defining moments in her life, from her difficult childhood to her multiple miscarriages.

"It was not easy to talk about myself," she said honestly, "but it was the right risk to take. People told me that they felt closer to me and understood me better. Instead of making me seem to be a weak leader, as I had feared, it made people see me as more genuine and authentic."

It was so effective that Jodi scheduled a meeting with her 15-person leadership team, where she asked them to share stories about defining moments in their own lives.

"The whole group came together and we shared a lot," she said. "Since then, I've learned so much more about the people who work for me, what matters to them, and what motivates them. It has made us a better team. It helped me to see that by modeling vulnerability, I gave people permission to be vulnerable with me, with each other, and even with their clients." As she put it: "Vulnerability helps to build relationships."

———

WHAT JODI DISCOVERED WAS that, contrary to her expectations, she gained strength from sharing her story and being vulnerable with others. And she built trust by listening to other people's stories. I couldn't agree more. One of the most vivid examples of this phenomenon in my life occurred during a coaching session I was hired to conduct with employees of a long-established New York bank.

The bank's CEO asked me to meet with a group of its senior leaders to discuss the benefits of relationship building, corporate social responsibility, and community engagement. I was ushered into a sixth-floor conference room that had thick oak tables, plush leather chairs, and 19th-century European artwork on the walls. It was the sort of Old World room that exuded a sense of importance. As we began the meeting, I suggested we go around the table and have people introduce themselves and give me a brief overview of their current philanthropic activities. It was an impressive group—every person was involved in two or three charitable endeavors, and many of them sat on the boards of local nonprofits.

One of the last people to speak was a woman who appeared to be in her sixties. Her introduction of herself and her community activities was a sharp contrast to those that had preceded her.

"I'm not involved in anything, to be honest with you," she said. "I have been involved with community groups in the past, but I decided to stop. I just decided that I wanted to spend more time at home and with my husband, rather than to go out several nights a week to meetings."

Although I was a bit surprised by her blunt dismissal of community involvement, I said, half jokingly, "Wow, you must have a great marriage."

"Yes, I've been married for 40 years," she replied.

"That's incredible. Tell me a bit about your husband," I said.

As soon as the words were out of my mouth, this lady broke down crying, which startled everyone in the room. This wasn't a quiet cry, with moist eyes or tears trickling down her cheek, but a convulsive cry punctuated by sobs and gasps.

"Is something wrong?" I asked her gingerly.

"It's just that my husband is now 68 years old and nobody in his family, not his parents nor his siblings, has lived past 70. I feel like I'm in my last years with him. He's been my best friend for four decades and I want to spend as much time as I can with him. I want to enjoy time with him before it's too late. So that's why I pulled myself back from community activities. My husband is more important."

"Thank you for sharing that with us," I told her. "We should all be so lucky to have such a strong marriage that we're still best friends after 40 years."

The room was silent, and I could tell that no one quite knew how to proceed. I wanted to take advantage of the emotion of that moment, and so I asked the other people in the room, "How many of you in here knew your colleague's story before today?"

Not a single person raised a hand.

"Well," I said, "I'll tell you right now, if you want to be

a better team, one way to start is by getting to know each other. In fact, I'd like to hear more of this. We can get to know each other by sharing stories that are important to us, the stories that made us into the people we are today."

For the next hour we sat at that conference table and listened to tales about one another's lives. It turned out to be one of the most moving meetings I've ever participated in.

One of the tales that stayed with me, for instance, was from a woman who had watched a young boy die in her arms several decades earlier, when she worked as a pool lifeguard, and had been carrying around the anguished feelings with her ever since. "I wish I could have saved that kid," she repeated to us several times, still tormented by an event that had happened decades ago.

At the end of the meeting, I asked everyone again whether they had ever heard any of these stories before. No one had.

"This is an important lesson," I said, "not only about the power of sharing or of vulnerability, but of the power of knowing the people you work with. When you get to know another person in this way, it helps you understand them in a new way. It's not about exposing dark secrets—it's about understanding the life events that made people into who they are. When you know that, you start to accept people more unconditionally; you begin to understand what makes them tick. And it results in stronger and deeper relationships, personally and professionally.

"Remember," I told them, "everyone has a story."

INCH #10: VULNERABILITY

Each of us is on a unique journey, and sharing that unique narrative with others—even in work situations—is a sign of strength, not weakness. Heart-led leaders understand that transparency is the fastest way to foster trust, build teams, and grow relationships. Vulnerability is not about sharing secrets; it's about sharing insights into what makes you tick. It's the most contagious trait, because your willingness to share gives others permission to open up and share in return.

11. Love Your Enemy

———

I N THE FALL OF 1987 I WAS AN 18-YEAR-OLD STUDENT IN AN UP WITH People cast that visited the Fort Breendonk concentration camp near Antwerp, Belgium. It was not only my first visit to Europe but my first trip outside the United States. I have many cherished memories of traveling in Belgium, from the splendor of the Grand Place in Brussels and the medieval beauty of Bruges to the crisp taste of Belgian beer, *pommes frites*, and dark chocolate. But the experience that had the greatest impact on me took place at Breendonk. And the most memorable part of the experience was the time we spent with our tour guide, Frank, who had been a prisoner at that very camp during World War II.

Our visit to the concentration camp was deeply disturbing, as you might expect. We were appalled by the cold, cramped barracks, revolted by the torture chamber, and shocked into silence by the gallows and the firing squad area, where prisoners were executed. It was profoundly disturbing to reflect on the horrors that human beings are capable of inflicting on one another in the name of war and ideology.

Frank told of us being locked up with 4,000 other prisoners in an overcrowded train in the middle of winter before being incarcerated at Breendonk. He watched helplessly as some of his fellow captives perished over the succeeding days in a freezing rail car without food or water. At the prison camp, torture and summary executions were carried out in front of other prisoners, sometimes for no reason at all other than to set an example. The meals were pitiful—thin soup and tiny pieces of stale bread. And the malnourished inmates were subject to hard labor day in and day out. Frank told us about the time he could no longer wait for a bathroom break and urinated in a field as he worked. The guards responded to this by beating him unconscious and leaving him for dead. That night he came to atop a pile of dead bodies before managing somehow to crawl back to the barracks.

Miraculously, Frank survived the concentration camp and was freed when Breendonk was liberated by Allied forces. At the time he was set free, Frank said, his weight was down to 80 pounds. He was filled with venomous hate for every German he encountered. It took him years after the war to get over that hatred. But he did eventually recover his life, and he did so by surrendering to love and by learning to forgive. His new wife—a young woman he had courted before the war broke out—helped him to rediscover a sense of gratitude for life, he said, and he learned how to love again, one step and one day at a time.

"Just give love," he said to us. "Every day. That is the secret."

Frank had been through so much horror and had nearly been killed by the Nazis. Yet he could find his way to forgiveness. He had made room in his heart for love. Frank had, in essence, learned to hate the sin but love the sinner.

He dedicated himself to giving tours of Breendonk, in part because he didn't want the world to forget the unspeakable horrors that took place within those camps, and also because he wanted to tell anyone who would listen about the power of love and forgiveness.

"I beg you to learn to love each other," was Frank's plea to us that day. Three decades later, those words still echo in my head. They are forever etched on my heart.

I RECENTLY LEARNED ANOTHER lesson about the power of forgiveness from a woman who had to deal with a gut-wrenching decision in a situation that may hit a lot closer to home for many of us.

A friend of mine, Matthew West, an award-winning Christian singer, wrote a song called "Forgiveness" about the mother of a 20-year-old girl who was killed by a drunk driver in Pensacola, Florida.

A young man named Eric Smallridge, a recent graduate

of the University of West Florida, climbed behind the wheel of his car on May 11, 2002, after having a few drinks, as he may have done on many other occasions in his life. But this time his luck ran out. He hit another car, instantly killing Meagan Napier and her best friend, Lisa Dickson. He was convicted of two counts of DUI manslaughter and vehicular homicide and sentenced to 22 years behind bars in the Florida Department of Corrections. Eric's new identity was as inmate P22679.

Meagan's mother, Renee, spent several years consumed by grief and hate over the loss of her daughter. Then she realized one day that there was only one way to overcome the darkness in her life and to rise above the bitterness and anger she felt toward Eric Smallridge. And that was to forgive him. So she worked up the strength to get to know Eric and eventually to forgive him for the accident. Then she found the courage to go to court and ask a judge to reduce Eric's prison sentence.

Eric was eventually released from prison in 2012 after serving half of his original sentence. He and Renee now work through the Meagan Napier Foundation to make joint appearances before student groups around the country, speaking about the dangers of drinking and driving and about the power of forgiveness. They acknowledge that their relationship is hard for others to understand, but speaking together provides a way for them both to heal.

Frank and Renee have taught me that forgiveness is a leader's greatest opportunity to demonstrate love. If Frank can forgive the Nazis for their horrendous war crimes, if Renee can forgive the man who killed her daughter, then perhaps we are all capable of loving the unlovable and forgiving the unforgivable.

INCH #11: FORGIVENESS

Harboring ill will or negative feelings toward someone not only clouds our memory but also crowds our heart. The only way to make room for love, empathy, and compassion is to push hate and resentment out. Every leader, organization, and community deals with adversity and negativity. Those who find their way to forgiveness make room in their hearts for compassion and for the small kindnesses that lead us to acceptance, grace, and love.

12. "Just Read the Contents of the Vault"

WHENEVER I SPEAK FOR THE FIRST TIME TO A COMPANY OR GROUP, I try to learn as much as I can about the organization: I'll visit one of the manufacturing plants, meet with executives, or even spend a few hours working for the company. I've worked as a barista for Starbucks, as a waiter for Dave & Buster's, and as a call center employee for Convergys. The insight that I gain allows me to better connect with my audience.

This is how I first became acquainted with John Hayes, the CEO and president of Ball Corporation. Ball, a Fortune 500 company with 15,000 employees around the world, makes both recyclable metal containers (check your next soda or beer can for the little Ball logo) and aerospace technologies. When the company asked me to give the keynote at its annual leadership conference, I arranged to visit a bottling plant in Saratoga Springs,

New York, where I met with Steve DiLoreto, the plant manager.

Steve greeted me with a hard hat and safety glasses and gave me a tour to show me how aluminum cans are made. Later we attended the company's monthly employee barbecue before heading back to Steve's office, where he answered my questions. What struck me most about my time with Steve was the incredible respect he held for the company's CEO, John Hayes.

Steve told me a story about a visit John had recently made to the Saratoga Springs plant. It's not unusual, of course, for a company president to visit factories, stores, or other sites to check on operations or to meet with employees. In many cases, the CEO flies in on a corporate jet or drives over in a limousine, surrounded by an entourage of aides, and perhaps does a perfunctory meet-and-greet with employees. But when John inspects a plant, he usually drives himself there, goes directly to the plant floor to ask questions, and almost always visits on a day when the company barbecue is scheduled so that he can eat lunch with employees and listen to everyone's complaints, comments, and suggestions.

John says these encounters help him to connect with employees as people and to foster the sense of family that he strives to cultivate throughout Ball Corporation.

"Do you want to work for a boss who gets picked up in a fancy limousine while he is making decisions to lay off workers?" John asked. "I always try to remember that these jobs affect people's livelihoods, their families, their

dreams. It doesn't mean that you don't make tough decisions if you need to, but at the same time you have to have
empathy."

I was intrigued by John's management style. So I asked
John if I could spend some time with him at Ball's corporate headquarters in Broomfield, Colorado. When I
walked the halls to his office, I saw framed posters of a
company-wide initiative called Drive for 10, which empha-
sized three messages: "We know who we are," "We know
where we are going," and "We know what is important."
John told me that when he became CEO in 2011 the company was already thriving; he wanted to keep steering it in
the right direction. So they came up with a campaign to
link present goals and future ambitions to the firm's heri-
tage and culture.

"You have to know who you are in order to understand
where you've come from, where you're going, and what
you're doing," he said. It was then I discovered that John
Hayes not only understands but lives one of the main principles of heart-led leadership: *if you put the who first, you'll
achieve more what.*

John's awakening was similar to my own: he realized one
day that he wasn't satisfied with his life or passionate about
his work. In the 1990s he had a successful job in corporate
finance at Lehman Brothers in Chicago, but he wasn't all
that excited about getting out of bed each morning.

"That is when I realized that you've got to love what
you do," he told me. "We spend more waking hours at
work than we do at any other activity, and it astounds me

how many people go through life not loving what they do and who they do it with."

So John left the financial industry and went to work for Ball Corporation. Eleven years later he became the company's CEO and president. Today he thinks of Ball as a family.

"Families play together and families fight together, but families always have each other's back," he says. It's a sentiment that is important to him. "I was born into a family that, candidly, was not a family. Yes, we were all of the same blood, but we didn't have this mind-set of what it really, truly means to be a family, a team."

John first experienced what it was like to be part of a family when he was on a school hockey team. "My hockey teammates were my surrogate family when I was in high school," he says. And although he has a family of his own now, he considers Ball Corporation his family as well. "I'd like my employees to feel that way, too."

In speeches to his staff, it is a refrain that John constantly repeats. "We are a family. We are a team," he says. "To me, these words are interchangeable. The whole is far greater than the sum of the parts."

He believes one of the primary responsibilities of a leader is to help give employees a sense of purpose and show them that they are working for something greater than their individual jobs. "People want to be part of something bigger than themselves," he told me. "I think companies have an opportunity to provide that, and it astounds me how few companies really get it. The role of a leader is not to be the smartest person in the room but to help people connect to that higher purpose."

John has an unusual tool to help keep himself and the Ball family connected to its higher purpose: a briefcase. But this is no ordinary briefcase. He calls it the "Ball vault," and it holds a collection of work-related materials that remind him of what is most important at Ball.

"Things like thank-you notes from plant people, old speeches and company videos, notes from people thinking we can do better, and notes from people just wanting to be heard," he said. "I often say that when they cart me out of here, I have just one request for whoever replaces me: 'Prior to making any meaningful decision, just read the contents of the vault. You will see perspectives that you didn't know existed. You will see passion that cannot be quantified. And you will see an accumulation of culture that you will find nowhere else.'"

"And why is that important?" I prodded him.

Without hesitation, John responded, "Because once you figure out who you are, it will dictate what you want to do and where you are going."

INCH #12: PURPOSE

One of the primary roles of a genuine leader is to help connect people to a higher purpose. John Hayes says it best: "People want to be part of something bigger than themselves." A good place to start is by emphasizing these three messages: Know who you are, know where you're going, and know what is most important.

13. I Believe in You

———

N 2012 I SPOKE AT THE NATIONAL GAME CHANGER COACHES LEADER-
ship Summit at the American Airlines Center in Dallas,
along with a number of athletes and celebrities. In my
speech, I told the audience about an individual who was
a game changer in my life: Bob Veltidi, my varsity football
coach at Suffern High School. I played high school football for only one year, but in that one year Coach Veltidi
had a significant impact on my life that persists to this day.

I wrote about my high school football experience in
my first book, *It's Not Just Who You Know*, so I won't repeat
all the details here. But here is the backstory in a nutshell.
Coach Veltidi invited me to try out as a kicker for the varsity football team at the end of my junior year. I had been
on the baseball, soccer, and ski racing teams and was just
an average athlete. The coach knew I was destined to be
a reserve on the soccer team that fall, and he told me he
needed a kicker. He also said that he needed players on

his team who were leaders. When I told him I'd be willing to give it a shot, he gave me a quick lesson in kicking, then handed me a bag of footballs and a kicking tee and told me to be ready for tryouts in August. Before I left his office, he looked me in the eye and recounted the most magical words any coach can say to a player: "Tommy, I believe in you."

I practiced my heart out all summer long and, after learning to kick a football through the uprights from 30 yards away, I won the job as the starting kicker for the team. That team turned out to be one of the greatest in Suffern High School's history, largely because our quarterback, Danny Munoz, was one of the best in the state. After winning our first seven games of the season, we entered a showdown with our archrivals, undefeated Clarkstown North. With 29 seconds left in the game, we found ourselves trailing by two points, 21–19, and staring at a fourth down on the Rams' 20-yard line.

Coach Veltidi motioned the kicking team onto the field. I gulped. I had spent most of the season kicking extra points; now I was faced with a 37-yard field goal attempt in the last seconds of the game. If I missed, our team would no longer be undefeated. My heart was in my mouth as I considered the stakes. The opposing coach called time out to "ice" the kicker. As I stood on the field contemplating the moment, Coach Veltidi came up and put his hand on my shoulder.

"Spaulding, I asked you to be on this team because I believed in who you are as a person, not just as a player," he said. Then he grabbed my face mask, pulled me in close, and once again repeated the four words every player wants to hear from the coach: "I believe in you."

Those words rang in my ears as I lined up for that field goal attempt, and they ring in my ears even today. Believe it or not, I made that kick, and we won the game 22–21. My teammates carried me off the field. The next day's *Journal News* had a banner headline in the sports section: "Suffern Wins on Spaulding's Kick."

I still think about that kick a quarter century later. Not because we won the game, or because of the accolades I received. But because I justified the belief my coach had in me. It gave me the confidence to overcome other obstacles in my life. All because someone believed in me.

When I was invited to speak at the Game Changers Conference, an audience of thousands of high school coaches, the first person I thought of inviting to join me was my father, who is my biggest fan (he has watched the video of that kick about a thousand times since I graduated from high school). The second person was Coach Veltidi, who had since retired.

I tracked down Coach Veltidi's phone number, called him, and invited him to Dallas to attend the conference as my guest. Although I think of Coach Veltidi often, I had seen him only once since high school. And I felt as though I'd never properly thanked him for how he shaped my life. Coach Veltidi graciously accepted my invitation, not knowing that I had a grand plan in place to thank him publicly.

So, with Coach Veltidi in the audience at the Game Changers conference, I shared my football story with the crowd. I challenged them to consider that while good coaches may win games, great heart-led coaches build a legacy of leaders around them, on and off the field. I played a video of the kick, and I talked about the impact Coach Veltidi had on my life.

At the end, I introduced Coach Veltidi to the audience and asked him to stand and be recognized. And I thanked him for being the game changer in my life. The place went crazy; he received a standing ovation from the thousands of other coaches in attendance. He later told me that it was one of the greatest moments of his life—it meant so much for him to hear about the impact he had as an educator, and to know that he was able to so profoundly affect even one person's life.

As I looked into the audience from the stage, I could see my father and my coach sitting side by side, tears in their eyes. And I realized at that moment that, to me, having a chance to thank and honor my coach publicly was even more important than my kicking that game-winning field goal twenty-eight years earlier.

INCH #13: ENCOURAGEMENT

I believe in you. They are among the most beautiful words you can say to someone. But how many people in your life or organization actually hear that from you? And how often do they hear it? The word *encouragement* means "to bring courage to others." When you encourage people—when you show trust in them—you are giving them the courage and fortitude to go beyond their own expectations for themselves. Heart-led leaders realize that encouraging others is a game-changing opportunity, both for the leader and for the person who is encouraged to do something great.

14. When a Boss Is More Than a Boss

WHEN I FIRST MET MARGIE TLAPA, SHE WAS THE ASSOCIATE VICE president for corporate relations at Ashford University, where she oversaw a far-flung team of about 70 people. Margie's staff worked with corporations that wanted to help their employees attain a degree from Ashford's online education program. The campus is based in Iowa, but Margie worked out of an office in San Diego (the headquarters of Bridgepoint Education, Ashford's parent company), and her staff was scattered across the country.

Of course, Margie understands full well the value of building relationships. Not only did she work every day to foster relations with corporate clients, but she was also responsible for maintaining rapport among a team that didn't even work together in the same building. And Margie is more than just a leader who manages a team—she is a loving presence in their lives. I have seen firsthand the

strength of the bonds that exist between Margie and her
team members.

A few years ago Margie invited me to keynote her semi-
annual team meeting in San Diego. There was a dinner
banquet prior to the speech, and I was seated next to a
beautiful African American woman named Michelle from
Los Angeles, who had a contagious, warm smile. Michelle
was a delightful person, and I enjoyed getting to know her.
I was shocked during our conversation to learn that she
had been diagnosed with stage four cancer. The doctors
had told her she had only another 12 to 18 months to live.
Margie was the only person on the team who knew about
her diagnosis. Michelle had asked Margie not to disclose
this information because she wanted to enjoy her time
with her colleagues without the sadness of saying goodbye.

As we talked, Michelle told me her fears. She was afraid
of dying, of course, but she was more afraid of what her
death would mean to her six-year-old daughter. You see,
Michelle was a single mother. In spite of her illness, Michelle exhibited a strong spiritual faith and a genuine passion for life. When I asked her what she wanted to do with
the time she had left, she said she would like to spend as
much time as possible with her daughter. It was difficult
to do, given her work schedule and the cancer treatments
she was receiving, she said, but if at all possible she'd like
to be home more. She also dreamed of taking her daughter to Disneyland.

I was so taken aback by Michelle's story that the following day I talked to Margie and offered to help in what-

ever small way I could. I put her in contact with my friend Lee Cockerell, the former executive vice president of operations at Disney and the best-selling author of *Creating Magic*. Lee agreed to arrange a special day at Disney for Michelle and her daughter, including a magical night in the Cinderella Castle Suite. Margie took over from there.

She handled the details for the event at Disney, including raising money to help pay for the visit. Margie could have easily stopped there, knowing that she'd helped create a lasting memory for Michelle and her daughter. But Margie wanted to do more. So she went to her bosses with an idea for a new policy that would allow employees to donate vacation time to a co-worker.

After receiving company approval for her proposal, Margie (with permission from Michelle) sent an email to her team, informing them about Michelle's condition and the new benefits policy. Within days, the team of 70 individuals responded not only with dozens of cards, baskets, and homemade gifts for Michelle but also with a year's worth of donated vacation time! Michelle now had a full year of paid time—time that she could devote solely to her daughter and to her cancer treatments, without the stress of worrying about work, bills, or health insurance. If the worst-case scenario came to pass, Michelle's daughter would at least have had the chance to spend time with her mom during that final year.

It was one of the most powerful examples I've seen of generosity at work. The example set by Margie and her team inspired Bridgepoint's executives to later put in place a permanent policy enabling anyone in the organization to donate vacation time to someone in need.

"This couldn't have happened if we hadn't all felt we could love one another in that way, not just as co-workers but as family," Margie told me. "It all started from the original idea of caring for one another in ways that go beyond the traditional work culture."

Michelle still is in a battle for her health and her life, but she has outlived her original prognosis, and there is hope that she'll survive. I don't know if the time off work and the time spent with her daughter improved her health, but I wouldn't be surprised if they did. What I do know is that none of this would have happened without the generosity of her co-workers, or without the determined leadership, empathy, and love of Margie Tlapa.

When I spoke to Margie not long ago, she told me there were actually two gifts that came out of this experience. One, obviously, was helping Michelle. But the experience also had a positive impact on the entire workplace culture of her office.

"Employees started connecting with one another in a deeper, more meaningful way," she said. "The catalyst for that change was the situation with Michelle. Afterward, people felt more comfortable in sharing their lives with one another. It shifted the dynamic of our team. We cared about hitting our goals as much as before, but we also started looking out for one another more. It's shocking how many people are going through challenges in their lives but never feel they're allowed to share it with people at work. This situation seemed to give people permission to share. I learned so much about the people on my team. It was a beautiful experience. It helped me realize that when people feel cared for, they're even more productive. Why can't our work lives be like that all the time?"

INCH #14: EMPATHY

Empathy is more than an expression of sympathy or kindness toward someone—it's a deeper sense of understanding and a more heartfelt connection to the feelings and emotions of others. Empathy makes an act of kindness more than a transaction. When heart-led leaders act with empathy, they inspire others to do the same. And when people feel empathy, their attitude and outlook improve. In my experience, people who feel cared for are more productive employees, more supportive of colleagues, and more responsive to customers.

15. A Culture of Giving

———

NOT LONG AGO I SENT AN EMAIL TO ABOUT 50 FRIENDS ASKING IF they could identify the following five men: John Tyler, Millard Fillmore, Chester Arthur, Benjamin Harrison, and Franklin Pierce.

The answers that came back included "the offensive line for the Denver Broncos" and "partners at a law firm."

Nope and nope. Well, all five were at some point lawyers, but not in the same firm.

Here's a hint. They have something in common with these five men: George Washington, Thomas Jefferson, Abraham Lincoln, Franklin Roosevelt, and John F. Kennedy.

The second five, of course, were U.S. presidents. So were the first five.

If you didn't recognize those first five names, don't feel bad. If it weren't for the U.S. presidents place mat that sits under my son Tate's plate at our kitchen table, I wouldn't have known that Chester Arthur was the 21st president of the United States (1881–1885).

Tyler, Fillmore, Arthur, Harrison, and Pierce all were one-term presidents, and Tyler, Fillmore, and Arthur reached that office only because they were serving as vice president when Presidents William Henry Harrison, Zachary Taylor, and James Garfield died in office. All of these individuals were probably good men, but their accomplishments as presidents were minimal.

Now think about the other five men I mentioned: Washington, Jefferson, Lincoln, Roosevelt, and Kennedy. These leaders faced extraordinary challenges and were able to achieve extraordinary results. You don't even need their first names to recognize who they are. We name streets, schools, towns, and airports in their honor. All, with the exception of JFK, who was assassinated in his first term, were elected to multiple terms as president. And they had a significant impact on U.S. and world history.

My point about John Tyler, Millard Fillmore, Chester Arthur, Benjamin Harrison, and Franklin Pierce is that it takes more than a title to create a legacy. Titles mean little unless they are accompanied by ideas and actions that make a difference in people's lives. And if the measure of our legacy is the difference we've made in other lives, then a young girl named Alexandra Scott left a legacy that measures up to or even outshines that of a few former U.S. presidents.

Alex was a young girl from Connecticut who, not yet one year old, was diagnosed with neuroblastoma, a childhood cancer. She spent several years undergoing medical treatment, including a stem cell transplant that was performed the day after her fourth birthday. As Alex was recovering from that procedure, she announced to her mom that after leaving the hospital she intended to open a lemonade stand. Her goal was to help other children who had cancer by raising money for research. She said that she wanted doctors to be able "help other kids like they helped me."

Alex followed through on her goal; she opened her lemonade stand later in the year, with help from her family. By the end of the first summer, she managed to raise $2,000 for cancer research selling glasses of lemonade from the front yard of her home. For the next few years Alex and her family continued to operate this simple drink stand. As news trickled out about this dedicated little girl who was intent on helping others even as she continued to fight her own battle with cancer, more people joined the cause and opened their own lemonade stands in support of Alex's dream. Within four years, that one stand turned into a lemonade stand movement that raised more than $1 million for cancer research.

I'm sad to report that Alex lost her battle with cancer and passed away at the age of eight. But her parents and brothers continue her work through the Alex's Lemonade Stand Foundation. To date, the organization has raised an incredible $80 million. Yes, $80 million—that is not a typo. That, my friends, is a legacy. One young girl battling a deadly disease opens a modest lemonade stand in her front yard and ends up launching a nationwide drive against childhood cancer.

But you don't have to be a president, a philanthropist, or the founder of a national nonprofit organization in order to make a difference in the world. And you don't have to be wealthy. Nor do you have to be famous. You don't need to have a show on television or a weekly column in the newspaper. You just need the desire to give.

I DISCOVERED SOMETHING ABOUT the astonishing power of generosity a few years ago, when I was asked to keynote a biennial meeting of franchisees of Jersey Mike's Subs. The company's leaders asked if they could meet with me ahead of time so I'd have a better understanding of their business. Of course I said sure—I always like to learn as much as I can about an organization before giving a talk. So I arranged a meeting in Washington, D.C., as I happened to be in town. I had no idea at the time that this was going to be one of the most memorable get-to-know-you meetings I'd ever had.

My first hint of Jersey Mike's distinctive corporate culture came when Peter Cancro, Jersey Mike's founder and CEO, Hoyt Jones, the company president, and John Teza, the chief development officer, drove three and a half hours from their corporate headquarters in Manasquan, New Jersey, to pick me up at my Washington hotel. We got into Peter's car—with Hoyt driving and Peter in the backseat with me—and drove another hour to a Jersey Mike's franchise in Maryland, where we sampled several of their sub sandwiches.

How many CEOs would devote 10 hours of their precious time to personally picking up a keynote speaker who was scheduled to talk to franchise owners in order to help him understand the company? What the Jersey Mike's team really wanted was for me to understand—to experience—the Jersey Mike's culture, a culture that doesn't just revolve around food. The entire time I was with Peter, Hoyt, and John, they never once mentioned the words "sub sandwich." The only hint I had of the quality of their food came when we were seated at the sub shop in Maryland and I learned, as I sampled their sandwiches, that every Jersey Mike's location bakes its own fresh bread and slices its own fresh meat and vegetables. The rest of my time with these executives was spent talking about the other factor that makes Jersey Mike's unique: its culture of giving.

The company's mission—its ethos—has embraced service and social responsibility from the time Peter, then a 17-year-old high school senior, bought Mike's Subs in Point Pleasant, New Jersey, in 1975. From the beginning, he was determined to help support his community.

"I'm from a small, tight-knit town, and I was always impressed by local businesspeople who gave back to their community," Peter said. "They always gave unconditionally, and that's what I learned from." So when he began opening franchises in 1987 (and changed the name to Jersey Mike's), Peter passed along this philosophy to his franchisees, encouraging them to "support the community that supports you."

Today, every individual who joins the Jersey Mike's family does so with the understanding that he or she is making a commitment to give back to the community and to donate a portion of profits to charity. Whenever Jersey Mike's opens a new sub shop, the new owner goes door-to-door, passing out free-sandwich cards to thousands of employees of local small businesses. On the back of the card is information about a local charity the franchise is supporting. Customers are then invited to make a donation whenever they come in for a sandwich. At the end of the month, there is a public presentation of a check to that nonprofit.

This monthlong act of collecting donations is repeated every year in March at every Jersey Mike's shop. There is a designated "Day of Giving" at the end of the month, when a franchise donates 100 percent of its proceeds from the entire day of business. Through these activities, the company in the last four years has raised $7.5 million for more than 100 charities.

This is a big commitment for franchisees, and not every potential owner is up for it. "That's why it all starts with selecting the right franchisees," Hoyt told me. "We tell all of our applicants, 'This is a chance for you to be a successful businessperson and to build some wealth, but we also expect you to make an impact in your community. It's part of our culture. The more you thrive, the more you can give back.'"

When I met Jersey Mike's inner circle, they spent every

minute of our two hours together discussing the responsibility that they believe corporations have to give back
to their communities. They told me that they produce
unique beverage containers (known as "giving cups")
for franchisees that list each shop's charitable endeavors
in local cities and towns. They brought samples of these
cups with them to show me. The cups celebrate everything
from a children's hospital in Ohio to a bike ride for multiple sclerosis in California to the Wipe Out Kids' Cancer
organization in Texas.

Since that meeting with Jersey Mike's, I've discovered
other companies that have built the concept of giving into
their business model. Not as an add-on that offers a thin
patina of philanthropy, but as an integral part of the company's operations.

One of these businesses was founded by Blake Mycoskie, a young man with an entrepreneurial spirit and a
love for travel who decided to start a shoe business based
on the novel idea that he would give away one pair of shoes
to a child in need for every pair of shoes that he sold. He
called it the One for One model, and it was so successful
that TOMS Shoes has since expanded into eyewear and
coffee. For every pair of glasses purchased, TOMS gives
the "gift of sight" to one person through new prescription
glasses or medical treatment. And beginning in 2014, for
every pound of coffee purchased, TOMS provides one
week of clean water to someone in need. Today, TOMS is a
thriving business and has given away more than 35 million
pairs of shoes and helped restore sight to 250,000 people.

"Opportunities to give are all around us," says Peter Cancro, Jersey Mike's CEO. Those words could just as easily have come from Blake Mycoskie or the Alex's Lemonade Stand Foundation. "We just need to seek the opportunity to give. That's why our mission statement is 'Giving—making a difference in someone's life.' That's what we stand for as a company. And, oh yeah, we also happen to sell sub sandwiches."

INCH #15: GENEROSITY

There are two parts to generosity: the compassion that fuels a desire to make a difference, and the commitment that turns that compassion into action. Heart-led leaders take action. They act on the idea of "supporting the community that supports you." Anyone can sell a widget. Heart-led organizations don't just desire to build a business; they want to give back to the people they serve. Nothing better reveals who you are more than how you give to others.

16. Being Heard

—

A FEW YEARS AGO I LEARNED A DIFFICULT BUT IMPORTANT LESSON IN being honest and transparent in my actions and words. At the time, I was looking for a way to honor three people from my hometown, Suffern, New York. One of them was a man who was my greatest mentor growing up and who had passed away at the age of 84. The other two were high school friends who died much too young. After making some inquiries, I eventually found a service organization in Suffern that was willing to organize an event that would raise scholarship funds in the names of these three individuals. In exchange for their help in staging the fund-raiser, I agreed to donate my time as the emcee and keynote speaker.

Early on in the process, I was introduced to a woman who agreed to oversee the planning and logistics for the event. After meeting her, I believed that we could not have found a better event chair. This woman was beyond talented. She had more drive, energy, and passion than almost anyone I knew.

During the initial planning stages for our fund-raiser, I worked closely with this woman. We became well enough acquainted that she eventually felt comfortable in sending me a heartfelt email asking for my help with a personal situation. She had a very close friend, she told me, who was dying of cancer. It just so happened that her friend was a big fan of the New York Yankees. She asked if there was any way for me to get some signed memorabilia from the team as a gift for her friend.

When I first read her email my natural instinct was to find a way to help. But I realized that I wasn't the right person to make it happen. I do have a couple of contacts and relationships in the Yankees organization, but they are not strong enough to ask, say, a star like Derek Jeter to reach out to a person in need. And even if I did have such a relationship, I'm not sure I would have been comfortable in asking the team for that kind of a favor. So I decided to answer her, explaining why I didn't feel I was able to assist with her request, as much as I wanted to.

Unfortunately, I didn't respond immediately, in part because I felt bad that I couldn't fulfill her request, and in part because I was in the midst of a 20-city tour that kept me on the road for the better part of a month. But you can guess what happened when I didn't respond. It was the same thing that happens to many of us when we procrastinate: the days soon turned into weeks, and still I put off writing that email.

Well, I eventually received another email from her, telling me that she had decided to step down as chairwoman of our event. The fund-raiser was a huge undertaking, and I assumed she had taken on too many responsibilities. Perhaps, I thought, she needed more local volunteers to help. So I responded to her note and told her that I supported her decision. I said that it must be difficult for her to juggle everything, since she held a full-time job and was also maintaining responsibilities at home as a mother and a wife.

But her next email shook me to my core. She told me that she was resigning not because she was overwhelmed by the workload but rather because she had lost faith in me. She told me that she was incredibly disappointed in me; she had sent me a heartfelt request to help her dying friend, and I hadn't responded. She felt that I wasn't living up to the message I preached in my speeches and in my work—to help and serve others.

Her words devastated me. I cannot remember the last time I was so upset with myself.

But after I got over the initial pain, my next reaction was one of denial. I decided it was unfair of her to judge me as a person solely because I didn't respond to her email. She had no idea, I told myself, how difficult it is to travel extensively for a living, to manage all of the follow-up correspondence I get, and to try to be a devoted husband and father.

As I gained more emotional distance, however, I began to see her side more clearly. I realized that if someone takes the time to reach out to me with a personal and heartfelt request involving a cherished friend who is dying, the least I could do was to reply. She had put herself on the line, and in her eyes I had brusquely turned her away. In the end, I learned an invaluable lesson. No is an acceptable answer, but no answer at all is not acceptable.

IN A MORE POSITIVE way, I learned another invaluable lesson while I was the CEO and president of Up with People.

When I took over the organization in 2005, Up with People was in considerable turmoil. The nonprofit had gone through difficult times and had even closed down for a few years when it was on the brink of bankruptcy. This created a high level of disillusionment among many alumni and supporters of the program, who felt the leadership hadn't always been transparent about their challenges. I compiled a list of 100 alumni clubs around the world and committed myself to visiting each of them during my first two years on the job. I wanted to share with them my vision for the organization, and I wanted to be honest with them about what the company had done right and wrong in the past. I felt that I needed buy-in from our 20,000 alumni if Up with People was going to thrive and prosper in the future.

During those two years, I met with thousands of alumni. Some of the meetings took place in intimate settings that saw me sit down with 10 alumni in someone's living room, while other events had me standing on stage in a big hall in front of a crowd of hundreds. The most intense, nerve-racking, and passionate meeting I had, however, was with the German alumni club.

The Germans are enthusiastic supporters of Up with People and have one of the most active alumni clubs in the world. They are also very honest and direct and will always tell you exactly what they are thinking. That day I stood on a stage in front of several hundred German alumni and walked them through the organization's history, its successes and failures, its financial challenges, and my vision for the future. Then I answered questions for an hour.

The questions were brutally direct. I answered as honestly as I could; if I didn't know the answer, I said so and then I promised to find the answer. I couldn't tell for most of the afternoon if I was winning them over or not, as they sat there with stony expressions and fired question after question at me.

When the meeting was over and I had answered every question asked of me as truthfully as I could, the audience gave me a standing ovation. In fact, it was the most sustained and inspiring ovation I've received for any speech or talk I've ever given. I appreciated the response, of course, but I also understood that these alumni were not applauding me in particular—they were applauding my candidness. I had been as honest as possible throughout my talk, and I had also listened to their questions and concerns. Whether they liked all the answers or not, the alumni at least felt they had been heard. Honesty was the real winner that day. Later they organized a party with an alumni band, and I sat down and drank a few beers with everyone. It reminded me of my rugby days in college, when two teams would beat each other up on the field and then bond later over drinks.

The experience showed me that people simply want to hear the truth, even if it's difficult. It helped me realize as well that sometimes people just need to know that their voices are being heard. Because honesty isn't only about telling the truth; it's also about listening to the truth from others.

INCH #16: HONESTY

It's difficult to be entirely honest with others without allowing others to be honest with us. We can't let this get lost in the shuffle of our busy lives. After all, it's often the small things that matter most—whether it's stopping to listen to feedback or taking the time to respond truthfully to a heartfelt request.

17. When the Hatch Closes

WHEN I WAS SEVEN YEARS OLD, I TOLD MY FATHER I WANTED TO BE an astronaut when I grew up. To his credit, my dad didn't tell me how difficult it would be, how much math I'd have to learn, or how unlikely it was that I'd actually become an astronaut. He just looked at me and said, "OK, son, let's go buy a telescope. After all, if you want to be an astronaut, you'll need to know where you're going." Thanks to my father, I used that telescope for years, even though I eventually realized that I wasn't really cut out to be an astronaut.

A couple years ago I met Rick Searfoss, who is a real astronaut and a veteran of three space missions. He, too, told his father at a very young age that he wanted to go into the space program. But Rick was more serious about this dream than I was. His dad told him that many astronauts began their career in the military, often as test pilots, and so as a young boy Rick decided to pursue exactly that path. He received a degree in aeronautical engineering from the Air Force Academy, embarked on a military career, became a test pilot, and then, in 1990, achieved his dream of joining NASA as an astronaut.

It's not often that we are able to sit down with an astronaut and get a firsthand account of what it's like to journey into space, so I pummeled Rick with questions. He told me about floating weightless by the flight deck window as the sunrise broke over the Earth, or of the immense thunderstorms he saw moving across the planet.

"You definitely get the sense that we're all in this together," he said as he described seeing the Earth from space. "And you think, 'Wow, how did I get so lucky to be here?' Seeing the Earth from space is deeply moving. It's a gift [that] I wish could be given to everyone."

But the story that made the biggest impact on me was his description of what it was like to climb aboard the shuttle and blast into space. He had gone through this experience three times, first as a crew member, then as a pilot, and finally in 1998 as commander of the space shuttle *Columbia*. I knew that astronauts needed a great deal of intelligence and courage, but listening to Rick helped me appreciate the staggering amount of teamwork and trust required to make each mission a success.

Strong teamwork is required in most ventures, of course, but in the space program the stakes are magnified. At work, if your leadership team fails, your project might fail; you might even lose your job. But failure in space can mean the difference between life and death.

During Rick's final trip into space, his three daughters were 15, 12, and 3.

"We had been through this goodbye drill twice before," said Rick. "But the first time, the girls had little idea of the risks. It was more 'Bye, Daddy! Have fun! See you when you come back to Earth.' For the second mission, the oldest two, Megan and Liz, were beginning to appreciate that Dad was going off to do something kind of risky. By my third flight, Megan in particular had some real concerns. Daddy wasn't just headed out of town on a business trip. There was a real, albeit small, chance we'd never see one another again in this life."

Rick told me that he calmed down when he settled in that night with his team at the Space Center because he knew they were exceedingly well prepared. "I looked at my crew and said to myself, 'Yep, I'm glad to trust my life to each of them.'"

I asked Rick to talk me through the experience of being launched into space.

"It starts to get surreal in the van out to the launchpad," he said. "You're in your flight suit, sitting with your crewmates, starting to understand this isn't a dress rehearsal. Then you get out of the van and you're dwarfed by this amazing, massive piece of human engineering. You get a lump in your throat, thinking, 'Wow, I'm actually going to climb onto that thing.'"

That "thing" includes the orbiter, which is the size of a large airliner attached to three rocket engines, plus an external engine and two solid rocket boosters. Sitting on the launchpad, the entire stack is a little under 200 feet high and weighs more than 4 million pounds. For the flight in which he served as commander, Rick had his crew pause after getting out of the van "so they could ponder the magnificence of what they were about to do and to recognize the collective effort of all the people who made the mission possible."

On the launchpad, the crew is accompanied by a handful of technicians who take them up the elevator and help them into the cabin. Once the astronauts are strapped inside, the technicians leave the site. The astronauts are now on their own, sitting atop millions of pounds of fuel that will soon blast them away from Earth.

"On the launchpad, your emotions are a combination of everything you can imagine," Rick recalled. "You're as excited as the night before Christmas when you're a kid; you're more nervous than before your final exams. Part of you is thinking, 'I could die in the next few minutes,' and the other part of you is thinking, 'This is the coolest thing ever!'

"In my last flight, as the commander, I took a quick glance out the window just after launch during the 'roll program.' It was a gorgeous spring day, and I could see massive crowds of people and a line of campers down the causeway. I also caught a glimpse of the building a few miles away where my family was watching from, and I just thought, 'Man, I hope this goes all right.'

"Soon, though, the emotions go away and it's all business. You get focused. Five minutes before launch the pilot turns on the auxiliary power units and the vibrations start. After that, you lower your visor and all you can hear is the whoosh of your own breathing."

Half a minute before launch, the onboard computers take over the launch sequence. The shuttle's main engines ignite with just under seven seconds to go, followed by the solid rocket boosters.

"Then it's just shake, rattle, and roll," Rick said. "There is a lot of vibration. My nerves go away because there is no turning back. I'm either going to be in space and weightless in eight and a half minutes, or there will be a malfunction and I'll be someplace else."

The solid rocket boosters propel the shuttle toward space for the first two minutes before being jettisoned at an altitude of 28 miles. After that, the shuttle's engines provide the thrust that accelerates the spaceship into orbit six minutes later at a speed of 17,000 mph. The external tank then separates from the orbiter and burns up in the atmosphere.

For two of Rick's three flights, this process played out smoothly. On the second launch, though, when he was the pilot on *Atlantis*, things didn't go exactly according to plan.

"We were 150 miles high, going 12,000 miles per hour and accelerating, when suddenly the warning alarm went off and our systems display started blinking an error message. Mission Control says, '*Atlantis*, we show a system three hydraulic leak. Pilot, execute hydraulic leak procedure.' I verified the onboard data and, sure enough, hydraulic fluid was draining. The shuttle's 'power steering' has three hydraulic systems and it works fine with two of them, so I just had to isolate the leaking system.

"I had performed that same procedure hundreds of times in simulators and could've done it in my sleep. The thing is, though, you have to do it while wearing a bulky glove, and the three isolation switches are only about an inch apart. And the shuttle may work fine with two hydraulic systems, but not with one. So flipping the wrong switch means game over. We were all just an inch away from dying if I had shut down the wrong system. And corkscrewing through the sky at 20 times the speed of sound is not how I wanted to end my day, or my life.

"Well, I quickly completed the procedure and I don't think my heart rate even increased. But about a minute later, it struck me what had just transpired. The hydraulic problem was handled, the adrenaline jolt was over, and now my nerves felt free to jangle a bit! I realized that this time it was not a simulation."

I asked Rick what it was like for him, knowing that he held not only his own life but the lives of the entire crew in his gloved hand.

"This is all enabled by trust," he said. "Not only trust in the crew, but trust in all of the people who have been involved in making this happen.

"It really hits you on the launchpad, when you crawl into the cabin, strap yourself into your seat, and then they close the hatch. When you hear it close, you realize, 'Now I really am in the hands of others.' Your crew, of course,

but also the team in Houston and the efforts of the thousands of people who are involved in the space program.
You know they all poured their hearts and souls into making this mission a success. And they're trusting you as well.
They're trusting you not to make a mistake."

How do you build the kind of team to which you can
literally trust your life?

Just as with any organization, he told me, it starts with
hiring the best staff and then getting your team as prepared as possible.

"It starts with recruiting," Rick said. "NASA simply does
not hire B players. And everyone is aware of the stakes, so
we all take our training seriously.

"For instance, there was one long simulation drill we
did that took out our computers. Basically we were dead
if we couldn't resurrect them, reload software, and figure
out where we were in orbit. When the lead trainer de-
briefed us, he said we had passed and been 'within the
parameters.' But I was not pleased with my own performance. So I bit the bullet. 'My performance was unaccept-
able,' I said. 'We're going to need to repeat this one. I'll
dive back into the books.'

"These all-day simulations are expensive and time-
consuming, but I didn't want to risk my life or the rest
of my crew because I was a poor student. I spent the next
week poring over computer manuals to get up to speed.
When we had our do-over, we passed with flying colors.

"So if you—as a leader—want to build trust, you have
to be as accountable to your team as you expect them to

be to you. They knew I had their back and they did every-thing they could to be sure they had mine.

"Because when that hatch closes, it's all about trust."

INCH #17: TRUST

Trust is at the heart of every great relationship and every strong team. A lack of trust, on the other hand, can easily destroy a team. Heart-led leaders know that trust is a product of preparation, collaboration, and shared responsibility. Everyone's contribution is critical. And the sense of accountability and trust demonstrated by the team's leaders builds the foundation and shows the way.

18. The Heart of a Turnaround

I N NOVEMBER 2008 WALT RAKOWICH WAS OFFERED A JOB AS THE CEO
of Prologis, an S&P 500 global real estate company
with operations in 22 countries. In most similar cases this
would be cause for celebration. Walt had worked at Prologis, which specializes in owning and leasing distribution
warehouses, for 15 years, making his way up from a marketing job to chief financial officer and then to president
and chief operating officer.

However, this was not the most auspicious time to be
moving into the corner office. It was the height of the
global financial crisis, and Prologis was suffering from a
plummeting economy and from its own management
mistakes. The company was in financial free fall. Its stock
price had tumbled 95 percent during the previous year,
and its market capitalization had fallen from $20 billion
to less than $1 billion. Walt had actually resigned from
the company earlier that year because of disagreements

over how the company was being managed, but when the board of directors finally dismissed the previous CEO, he heeded a call to return.

To most people, Walt's task of engineering a turnaround seemed doomed from the start. On the day he became CEO, the company's projections anticipated that it would be forced into bankruptcy in less than four months. Walt and his staff at Prologis reorganized the company, raised new equity, found ways to increase cash flow, and eventually paid off more than $10 billion of debt. Then, in 2011, Prologis and AMB Property completed the real estate industry's largest merger to date—meaning that Walt's tenure as CEO was an unqualified success.

But that's not what makes Walt's story unique. For me, the remarkable part of this tale is that Walt Rakowich turned around Prologis by using the principles of heart-led leadership. And he did it from the very first day he became CEO.

Bill Sullivan, who was the chief financial officer for Prologis at the time, recalls flying to New York for a meeting with investors within days of the company's leadership change.

"There had to be 400 people in that room, and another 1,000 in anterooms," he said. "You have to understand that the culture of communication prior to Walt coming on was 'Everything is rosy.' It was always good news. But now our stock had collapsed—it fell from $60 a share down to about $2.50—and all of the investors were mad. They wanted to know why this was happening. It was ugly.

"Well, Walt went in there and was completely open and transparent about everything. He went through a litany of financial mistakes the company had made and laid out a game plan for the coming months. He didn't want anyone's sympathy. There was no glossing over the facts. I don't think anyone had ever been that transparent with those investors before. They walked away knowing that we understood the situation we were in."

A few days later Walt presided over another meeting, this time with employees. According to Bill, Walt was just as candid with the company's employees as he had been with investors. He had to tell the staff that nearly one-third of them would probably be laid off.

"He stood there for maybe an hour and a half and answered questions as honestly as anyone could. People asked tough questions and some of them vented over decisions the company had made, but Walt was up front about everything. You could sense a momentum shift because the staff got straight answers and they could see we had a plan."

It's hard to imagine a more difficult first week on the job.

"Walt won back the support of our investors and our employees with heartfelt honesty," Bill told me. "His talk was straight up, but it was also straight from the heart. That's what won everyone's admiration. It's true that we made some good financial decisions after this, but if Walt hadn't made the heartfelt impression he did on those initial meetings, then nothing else would have mattered. I don't think we would have had a chance."

I wanted to know more about how Walt had accomplished the Prologis turnaround. He told me the cornerstone of his management style was to be "humble, honest, and human" and that he tried, most of all, to "lead with a heart."

"Humility," he said, "does not mean being weak. It's about having the confidence to listen and to respect the opinion of others. It's about being vulnerable. It's about encouraging and empowering folks and making sure they get the credit. Honesty is not only about being truthful but also about being transparent. It's about communicating even when you don't think you need to.

"And being human means being genuine and caring for others, no matter our position or the job that we do. For us, it also meant emphasizing corporate responsibility and community outreach initiatives. We wanted our employees to understand that we had a heart, even in the midst of difficult times."

I was impressed by Walt's determination to be so candid with his employees and shareholders. But I wanted to know why he felt it was so important to be so transparent.

"When transparency isn't there, trust breaks down," he said. "So, with our investors, we told them not to trust us but to watch us. In doing so we engendered their trust. We listened to what others had to say and made changes to our plan when needed. And we were transparent regardless of whether we had good or bad news to tell.

"With our employees, we told them everything we knew but were also honest about not having all the answers. Basically, we had an ongoing conversation with them through town hall meetings. It built trust. When I told our staff that we'd need to cut 30 percent of our workforce but that we didn't know who it was going to be yet, I knew there was a risk people would start leaving after that. But I thought it was more important to be honest with them. And when we did the layoffs, we tried to give people more than the typical severance package. We ended up hiring back some of the workers we let go, and I think they were willing to come back because of how we had treated them.

"The way I look at it is that leaders need to design an organization they would want to work for. There is no question in my mind that employees will begin to emulate you over time. So, for instance, if I want open communication from my staff, the only way to achieve it is to be that way myself. And if you treat people with dignity and respect and are transparent with them, you'll get respect back."

Walt then told me a story that illustrated how his willingness to be transparent and vulnerable as an executive was instrumental in forging new ideas and in getting people to work together toward a common goal.

"It was about one o'clock in the morning and 10 of us were meeting to discuss our financial condition," he said. "In that meeting, I was told that we would likely need to file for Chapter 11 bankruptcy protection during the next quarter. I remember feeling weak, and so I suggested taking a short break. As I walked down the hallway my legs started to feel like butter. I knew I had to find a chair, so I quickly entered a colleague's office. Unfortunately, just a few feet from a chair, I fainted. I hit my forehead on the corner of his desk, resulting in a pretty serious cut above my eye, a lump on my head, and a lot of blood on the carpet.

"Several minutes later I woke up and realized I had fainted and that everyone else was in the conference room waiting for me to return. So I did my best to stop the bleeding and then walked back to the meeting. Of course, they all noticed the cut on my head and wanted to know what had happened. I realized then that I was extremely vulnerable.

"I admitted to the group that our financial situation was too large for me to solve alone and that I needed their help. I said, 'Guys, I've been with this company for 15 years and I don't want to see it fail. But the truth is, I don't have all the answers.' I told them I was willing to listen to whatever ideas they had. And you know what? Although nothing was solved that night, everyone started working on it, and over the course of the next month we were able to overcome our challenges together. As a result, I came to understand that in leadership, there is power in vulnerability.

"As I talk to other leaders," Walt said, "it is amazing to me how difficult it is for people of stature to show vulnerability. Many leaders climb the corporate ladder by showing they can make tough decisions. They do a great job of appearing to be strong and in control of situations. Bosses love to see decisiveness, and in most cases decisive thinking requires a confidence that is convincing to others. And, of course, rarely is confidence associated with vulnerability. Don't get me wrong. I love confident people and it's one of the traits I looked for in promoting employees. But leadership is not about having the answers to everything. Real leadership comes from making mistakes, showing vulnerability by admitting your mistakes and then learning from them. You see, what most people want in a leader is someone they can relate to. People want to humanize their leaders. Showing vulnerability allows that to happen."

Transparency. Vulnerability. Leading with your heart. Humble, honest, and human. These are not the sort of words you expect to hear from a CEO on the topic of leadership or corporate turnarounds. Yet the end result of applying these values to the workplace, according to Walt, was that "our people gained a sense of purpose and worked even harder." And the company not only survived but ultimately thrived.

That is the essence of heart-led leadership.

INCH #18: TRANSPARENCY

To truly lead from the heart, you have to open yourself up and allow others in. Transparency goes beyond telling the truth. At its core, transparency is about being entirely candid about the facts regardless of the news, good or bad. And it's about willingly communicating insights about yourself and your business even when it isn't required.

PART THREE

LEAVING A *HEART*PRINT ON THE WORLD

One *Heart*print at a Time

WHEN I WAS A SOPHOMORE AT SUFFERN HIGH SCHOOL, I ATTENDED my older sister's graduation ceremony. I was proud to see Lisa receive her diploma, but there is another reason I'll never forget that June day in the auditorium of Rockland Community College.

You know the scene: the graduates stride across the stage, take their diplomas, shake hands with the principal, flick their tassels to the other side of their caps, wave to their families, pump their fists, and walk off into their future. This ceremony unfolded just as you'd expect— that is, until it was Michael Kosloski's turn to receive his diploma.

I didn't know Michael very well, but I had seen him around school. Frankly, he was hard to miss. Michael had muscular dystrophy, and to walk he needed help from the type of crutches that brace onto your wrists. Even with these crutches, he walked with such an extreme stagger that he had to laboriously move his hip in order to swing his leg in an arc and propel it forward. It was so painfully slow for him to walk that he had special permission to leave his classes 10 minutes early to get to his next class on time. School was obviously difficult for him, but I admired his desire to participate and his dogged persistence in getting through each day.

He showed that same tenacity at his graduation ceremony.

When they called Michael's name, he appeared on one end of the stage and slowly made his way to the other side, step by painstaking step. At first we all watched in silence, quietly urging him on. Then people cheered to encourage him. When he was halfway across the stage, he stopped to catch his breath, then began again. Soon everyone was on their feet and applauding. As the clapping grew in intensity, it felt more like a raucous football game than a graduation ceremony.

For those few minutes, the entire crowd's energy was focused on Michael's grit and determination. When he reached the principal and grasped his diploma in his hand, a big smile on his face, the crowd stood as one and the ovation was deafening. The walls shook with the thunder of our applause and encouragement. It was one of the most breathtaking moments I've ever witnessed—tears were streaming down my face.

Nearly three decades have passed since that graduation ceremony, and I'm still inspired by the memory of it. I vividly recall Michael's dignified determination, but I also will never forget how the audience responded. The auditorium that day reverberated with love as we cheered on Michael Kosloski. For a few minutes we all ceased thinking about ourselves and focused entirely on one individual.

I wonder sometimes what the world would be like if everyone would commit to taking time out of each day to focus our hearts entirely on one other person. Not for what we can gain, or how we can be more fulfilled, or how we can enhance our organizations. But for what we can give to others in both our personal and our professional lives. That, I believe, is the true essence of heart-led leadership. The 18-inch journey from the head to the heart is not just about us; it's also about other people.

Most of us spend our time fixated on a daily checklist of things to do—tasks to perform, goals to achieve—that symbolize the "what" achievements we've been taught to see as important in life. Instead of narrowly focusing our efforts on these things, I believe every person and organization should be looking to make a unique contribution each and every day, one that will create a lasting legacy. I call this our *heart*print—the distinctive identifiable stamp we can leave behind by sharing our heart with others.

I admit that I'm still in the process of learning and living these lessons. This is a journey that I'm taking every day, along with every one of you. For many years my life was focused almost entirely on that to-do list in my life. And although I'm immensely proud of my achievements and of the lives I've influenced, at some point in my journey I realized it wasn't enough.

Why? The deepest significance of heart-led leadership comes when you are able to put love at the center of everything you do. When love takes center stage, the focus of your life gradually shifts from yourself, your achievements, and the things on your to-do list to the desire to impact the lives of others. That is how you leave a *heart*print on the world.

I got a hint of this from Terry Adams, my first boss out of college. He taught me an invaluable lesson about the importance of finding the heart in others and investing in another person's success. What truly drove home this lesson, though, were relationships I developed with a young man and a young woman, Ethan and Nikki. They changed my life. They inspired me to become a better human being. I'm going to share their stories in the next few chapters because they helped me to understand that the best way to change the world is one life—one *heart*print—at a time.

The Circle of Who

———

WHEN I WAS ABOUT TO GRADUATE IN 1992 FROM EAST CAROLINA University, there was only one company I wanted to work for: Up with People. Because of the life-changing experiences that I had had as a student in Up with People five years earlier, my goal was to earn a staff position so I could give something back to the organization that had made such an impact on me.

So I sent in an application and three reference letters, and I was thrilled when the human resources department asked if I could interview with one of the company's vice presidents and cast directors while he was visiting central North Carolina.

During the days prior to that interview, I used up much of my savings to buy my first business suit, wing-tip shoes, a silk tic, and a leather briefcase. I went to the local Kinko's and printed my resume on expensive linen paper. I wanted this job more than I had ever wanted anything, and I was determined to do everything possible to make a great first impression.

I drove two hours to the Holiday Inn in Cary, North Carolina, for the interview. I walked into that meeting wearing the nicest clothes I had ever owned, carrying my brand-new leather briefcase, and feeling like a million bucks. So I was shocked to discover that the executive I met in the lobby was wearing jeans, tennis shoes, and a Minnesota Vikings football jersey.

"Hi, I'm Terry Adams," he said. "I hope you like *Monday Night Football,* because my Vikes are about to kick off."

With that, we walked across the street to a pizza joint to watch the game. Mr. Adams told me politely to lose the tie and briefcase and to call him Terry. The first "interview" question he asked me was "What kind of pizza do you like?"

Three hours later, I drove back to East Carolina University scratching my head.

"What the heck just happened?" I asked myself. It's not that I didn't like Terry Adams. In fact, we'd totally hit it off. He was the ultimate guy's guy, and he wore his South Dakotan values of midwestern humility right on his sleeve (or maybe I should say on his Vikings football jersey). But he hadn't asked me one question about my resume. He hadn't asked me about my grades in college. And he hadn't talked to me about Up with People or even discussed the position I was applying for.

When the football game ended and he walked me back

to my car, there was no mention of next steps or even a hint that maybe "someone from HR will be contacting you soon." Nothing. So I was a bit surprised two days later when I received a phone call from Beth Bowling in Up with People's human resources department. She told me that Terry Adams was also on the line.

"Are you near a refrigerator?" Terry asked me.

"Yes, I'm in my kitchen now," I replied.

"Do you have any beer in your fridge?"

"What college student doesn't keep a six-pack in the fridge?" I said.

"Well, pop open a beer and start celebrating," said Terry. "How would you like to be a part of our Up with People team?"

I was speechless—but only for a moment. I quickly accepted the position he offered me as an admissions representative on Up with People's road staff. A few weeks after graduation, I went to work for them.

Six months into that job, I made my first big mistake.

Terry was our cast director, and one day he asked if I'd like to introduce the Up with People show that night at a high school in Des Moines, Iowa. This was a huge honor, and it marked my very first public speaking opportunity with the company. My job was to thank and recognize the local sponsors, community service partners, and host families, and then welcome the audience to the show. It was only a three-minute speech, but it was an important three minutes.

I put on the same business suit I had purchased for my interview earlier that year and walked onto a stage in front of an audience of 1,500 Iowans. As soon as the spotlight hit my face, though, I froze. I was like a deer in the headlights and couldn't seem to get a single word out of my mouth. I forgot what city we were in. I forgot the sponsor's name. In the sweltering glare of that powerful spotlight, I could feel beads of sweat trickling down my face and I felt sick to my stomach. For what seemed like an eternity, I stood there speechless.

Thankfully, I was rescued by another staff member, Kimo Huddy, who put his arm around me and said, "I think what Tommy was trying to say is . . ."

I ran offstage as fast as I could, found the closest bathroom, and threw up. Later, I found an empty corner in the high school gymnasium, put my head between my legs, and bemoaned my very public failure. I vowed that I would *never* speak in public again. Ever!

The next day, we were preparing for our second Des Moines performance. I tried my best to avoid everyone involved in the show, fearing the previous night's fiasco would come up in conversation. Then Terry walked up to me and said, "Hey, Spaulding, you ready to introduce the show again tonight?"

"Are you kidding?" I said to him. "There is no way in hell I'm getting back on that stage."

Terry looked me in the eye and said something that I have since repeated to others at least a hundred times over the years. "Tommy," he said, "it is important that we make mistakes. That's how we learn and grow. Just don't make the same mistake twice."

That night I walked onstage to another packed auditorium. I had butterflies in my stomach, but I took a deep breath, and when that searing spotlight hit my face, I started to speak. Three minutes later I had completed the show introduction flawlessly.

I often wonder what twists and turns my life would have taken if Terry hadn't convinced me to introduce that second show—if he hadn't shown confidence in me and challenged me to face my mistakes and fears head-on. Would my life have somehow still led me to the career I have today as a leadership and motivational speaker? Or would I have stuck to my pledge to *never* speak in public again?

After working together that year, Terry and I not only stayed in touch but became the best of friends. In 2000, when I founded Leader's Challenge, Terry was our first CEO. In 2005, when I became the CEO and president of Up with People, I handpicked Terry as our chairman of the board. As the best manager I ever worked for, Terry was my first choice to help me turn around and lead Up with People. And so the man who was my first boss out of college then became the last boss I ever worked for, before leaving to embark on my own entrepreneurial ventures.

Some years later, I finally got around to asking Terry about that job interview at the pizza joint across the street from the Holiday Inn.

"Why didn't you ask me any questions about my resume or talk with me about the position I was applying for at Up with People?" I asked him. "And how did you know to hire me when all we did was to eat a pizza, drink a few beers, and watch *Monday Night Football*?"

"Tommy, a lot of the time in job interviews we focus so much on the small things, like what is on a person's resume, that we end up missing the big things, like what kind of people we're talking to or what is in their hearts," Terry said to me. "I didn't need to ask you any of the usual interview questions because I could tell just hanging out with you that you were special."

My point? If Terry Adams had paid attention only to the "what" questions, he might have noticed my lack of real-world business experience or my less than stellar academic record. And he might not have hired me. If he had focused on my first public speaking fiasco, he might not have given me a second chance. Instead, he kept his focus on the "who" questions. He believed in me, and by paying attention to who I was as a person, he changed my career and my life.

Terry taught me that being a Who Leader isn't just about putting your heart—your emotions, hopes, and dreams—at the center of your own life. It's also about finding the who and the heart in others.

TWENTY-TWO YEARS AFTER THAT horrible opening night onstage in Des Moines, I found myself in Denver preparing to deliver a short introduction during the opening event of the National Leadership Academy (www.nationalleader

shipacademy.org). The Academy, a successor to Leader's Challenge, is an annual national youth leadership conference that is run by my nonprofit, the Spaulding Leadership Institute. Every summer, since 2000, it attracts hundreds of high school students from around the country for an intensive four-day program that equips them with servant leadership skills, teaches them to become heart-led leaders, and inspires them to make a difference in their lives and their communities.

That day I was preparing to introduce Eric Blehm, the best-selling author of several books, including one of my favorite books of all time, *Fearless*, about how Adam Brown overcame tremendous odds to become a Navy SEAL. After reading *Fearless*, I reached out to Eric and told him how impressed I was with his book and with Adam Brown's story. We became fast friends, and I invited him to attend our Academy as a featured speaker.

As I was reviewing my introduction notes, I looked up and saw Lauren Adams, Terry's 16-year-old daughter and one of the students attending that year's National Leadership Academy. When I saw Lauren, it gave me an idea.

I asked Lauren and Eric Blehm to go for a walk with me around the tree-lined campus of the University of Denver, which hosts the Academy. As we walked, I told Eric and Lauren the story of my Up with People deer-in-the-headlights public speaking fiasco, but without mentioning the name of my old boss. Given my success as a public speaker, they were surprised by the inauspicious start to that part of my career. And they were touched by the heartfelt admiration I had for the boss who'd been so supportive of me two decades earlier.

"What a great story," Eric said.

I looked at Lauren and gave her the punch line.

"Lauren," I said, "the man who gave me a second chance and who has meant so much to me over the years is your dad."

Her eyes filled with tears.

"And the reason I asked you to take a walk with me," I told her, "is because I want to give you what your father gave me two decades ago—a chance. I'm supposed to introduce Eric tonight. But I think you should do the honors."

Looking like a deer in the headlights herself, Lauren nervously agreed.

Shortly before it was time for her to go onstage, I sat with Lauren in the packed auditorium. She was shaking with nerves, and I took her hand. "If you don't want to do this, you don't have to," I said. "I already have the introduction memorized, so I can still give it. But I want you to know, Lauren, that if you can do this, if you can get on that stage in front of hundreds of people and deliver this introduction, then you can do just about anything you want in life."

A few minutes later, with Terry and her entire family in attendance, Lauren delivered a flawless introduction of Eric Blehm. She didn't freeze in the spotlight, as I had done two decades earlier. I was as proud of her as if she were my own daughter.

So the story came full circle.

Terry Adams taught me what it meant to be a heart-led leader. He showed me what kind of impact leaders can have when they believe in others, when they see people for who they are and for what is in their hearts, and when they help every person strive to become something even greater than what they already are. I'm grateful that, 22 years later, I was able to honor and say thank you to Terry by helping to pass the torch to his daughter and a new generation of heart-led leaders.

Making a Wrong a Right:
Ethan's Story

─────

IN THE LATE 1990s, ETHAN FISHER WAS A RISING BASKETBALL STAR IN Colorado. A six-foot point guard, he was a two-time all-conference player at Poudre High School in Fort Collins who averaged 14 points and 7.5 assists per game as a senior in 1998. He attracted the attention of several Division I programs and seemed destined for a successful collegiate career. But Ethan had a secret. A secret that he'd managed to hide from even his family and closest friends. A secret that was destined to change his life in a way he could never have imagined.

Ethan was addicted to alcohol and drugs.

His addiction began innocently enough, with occasionally drinking beer or spirits with his high school buddies. But he soon discovered that he liked the feeling alcohol gave him. He was by nature an introvert, and the alcohol made him less shy and more confident about himself off the basketball court. So he drank more and eventually began experimenting with cocaine, Ecstasy, and other drugs. And then he just couldn't stop. The alcohol and drugs took over Ethan's life.

In a few years, his basketball career—and his life— spiraled out of control. From 1998 to 2003 Ethan was given an opportunity to play ball at five different schools. His athletic ability tantalized coaches, who gave him any number of opportunities, but Ethan self-destructed each time. He missed practices, drew the ire of coaches, and was kicked off several teams. He stopped going to classes and became ineligible to play. Strangely, though, his family and friends didn't seem to know why he was falling apart. Ethan didn't party in public, preferring to indulge his cravings alone, in private. So no one realized he needed help.

In the fall of 2003 Ethan was trying desperately to overcome his addiction and reform his life. He wanted to play basketball again and was taking classes at the University of Northern Colorado in an effort to become academically eligible to rejoin his college team. But midway through the semester, on the night of November 9, he attended a private party at a home in Fort Collins. He drank too much alcohol and then got behind the wheel of his Chevrolet Suburban to drive home. The next morning, he opened his eyes in a hospital bed. After he woke, a nurse came into his room.

"You're lucky to be alive," she told him. "Unfortunately, the man you hit head-on at 70 miles an hour was not as lucky. You killed him while driving drunk."

On the way home the night before, Ethan had had a blood alcohol content of .295 and had driven the wrong way down a four-lane road, head-on into another vehicle. The driver of the other car, a 57-year-old Fort Collins man with a loving wife and a daughter, died because he crossed paths with an out-of-control drunk driver. Ethan was convicted of vehicular homicide and sentenced to 10 years in prison. Not only was his basketball career over, but so was life as he knew it.

NEARLY A DECADE AFTER Ethan's accident, my wife and I purchased our dream home and moved our family to a new community on the outskirts of Denver. When it was time to move, I took a week off work so we could transfer our belongings to the new house, as well as paint rooms, do some remodeling, and take care of the necessary yard work. We did some of these tasks ourselves and hired contractors for other jobs, but we needed to do everything in just a few days. One morning, in the midst of this chaos, I received a phone call from a close friend, Marcel Pitton, general manager of the Brown Palace Hotel & Spa in Denver.

"Tommy, I have a favor to ask of you," he said. "I'm wondering if you could come downtown and have lunch with me. I have someone I'd like you to meet."

"Marcel," I said, "I have paint under my fingernails and contractors in my house, and my wife is upstairs unpacking boxes. It's not a great time, I'm afraid."

"I'll understand if you don't have time," he said to me,

"but this is a young man I'm trying to help. It's really important to me that he has a chance to meet you and he happens to be here with me now."

"OK, Marcel, I'll do it for you," I finally said, though I winced at the thought of telling Jill that I was abandoning her for a few hours in the middle of this busy day.

When I arrived at the Brown Palace for lunch, Marcel introduced me to a young man who was a graduate of Johnson & Wales University in Denver. He was a stellar student and had earned two degrees—one in entrepreneurship in 2010 (graduating summa cum laude) and another one in business administration in 2011 (graduating magna cum laude). He was also the sole recipient of that school's prestigious President's Award for outstanding academic achievement, character, and leadership.

His name was Ethan Fisher.

I didn't know anything about Ethan when I met him, so when I shook his hand I was surprised that he had trouble looking me in the eye. He spoke softly and seemed almost like a beaten dog that had been drained of confidence. I couldn't believe that this timid, insecure individual was the same impressive Johnson & Wales graduate Marcel was mentoring. When we sat down to eat, Marcel told me the young man had a story to share. Ethan then proceeded to tell me about his life, speaking almost in a whisper. I had to strain at times to hear him as he recounted for me every detail of his challenges with drugs and alcohol and his years in prison.

To be honest, it's not a story I would have wanted to

hear if I had known the details ahead of time. I don't have much sympathy for anyone convicted of DUI. My belief is that punishment for criminal behavior should be strict and uncompromising. If Marcel had told me Ethan's story on the phone, I probably wouldn't have wanted to meet him. But once at lunch, I had no choice but to listen to Ethan's story. And when I heard him speak and looked into his eyes, there was something about Ethan that won me over. I could tell he was a sincere individual who carried an enormous amount of guilt for what he had done.

After being convicted of vehicular homicide, Ethan spent three years in four Colorado prisons, in Denver, Buena Vista, Cañon City, and Rifle. He was then released into the custody of a halfway house for one year. For two more years he was under intensive supervised parole, which meant his movements were restricted, he had a 9:00 p.m. curfew, and he wore a monitoring bracelet on his ankle. This was followed by five years of standard parole, which included meetings with a parole officer and travel restrictions. Ethan was in the middle of this five-year parole when I met him.

After his release from prison, Ethan enrolled at Johnson & Wales University and joined the basketball team. He had to miss half the games because of his curfew and the prohibition against travel, but the team accommodated him. The chance to be part of a team again helped Ethan reconnect with his life. At school, he impressed everyone with his academic achievement and dedication to learning. He had remained sober since his accident and had worked diligently to reform himself.

Despite all of his hard work and achievements, life after prison was not easy. When he first looked for a place to live, he was turned away by 17 different landlords and apartment managers because of his felony conviction. It was only when a homeowner leased him a room in a private home that he could put a roof over his head.

Even harder for him to swallow was his inability to find a job. He loved to trade in the stock market and was very knowledgeable about financial investments. So he applied for a position at several financial firms. But most companies refused to even grant him an interview. Here was someone who graduated near the top of his class with two business degrees and a personal endorsement from the president of Johnson & Wales University but was rejected at every turn because of his criminal record. One company couldn't hire him because of his conviction. Another woman hung up the phone in the middle of a conversation when he told her about his prison time. Marcel, who had taken Ethan under his wing as a mentor, was prevented by corporate rules from hiring him.

The deck was stacked against Ethan—reentering society when you have been convicted of a crime is daunting and demoralizing. But Ethan's outlook shifted when he realized what he most wanted to do was to help other young people avoid the mistakes he'd made. He wanted to dedicate his life to telling his story and to teaching students that drinking and driving can destroy lives. Ethan was curious to know if I had any advice for him on how to get started, given my experience in public speaking.

I tried to reconcile my feelings about what Ethan had done with the person sitting across from me—a gentle, kind, remorseful young man. Ethan had been living with relentless guilt over the fact that he'd killed an innocent man. He had reached out to the victim's widow so he could apologize personally for shattering her life, but the woman refused to speak with him. She went so far as to obtain a restraining order against him, which prevented him from visiting certain parts of his hometown. When he was eligible for parole, she fought to keep him in prison.

"I don't blame her," Ethan told me. "I'd feel the same way. If someone killed one of my parents or siblings in a DUI crash, I'd have trouble forgiving that person, too. So I understand her feelings. I just wish I could tell her how unbelievably sorry I am."

A few hours earlier, before learning Ethan's story, I would have said he deserved to still be in prison for his actions. But seeing and hearing him in person, I felt a flood of compassion for him. I told Ethan that I wanted to help him with his speaking goals and his efforts to educate others about drunk driving, but that I couldn't. I told Ethan that until he forgave himself, he could not help others. Yes, a man had died, and a loving family had been shattered because of his actions. But if he truly wanted to make something positive out of this tragedy, I suggested, he would need on some level to forgive himself in order to move forward.

"Do you know you're forgiven?" I asked him. "You can't take back what you did. You can't bring that man back to life. But you're forgiven."

He looked down at his feet.

"Do you understand you're forgiven?" I asked him.

Again he refused to look at me.

"You are forgiven, Ethan," I said for third time.

His eyes filled with tears. I stood up and walked around the table and hugged him; both of us had tears streaming down our faces.

That lunch took place three years ago. I'm still not sure Ethan has fully forgiven himself. But I do believe he is on a path to redemption.

THAT NIGHT, I TOLD my wife about meeting Ethan. I couldn't fully explain my feelings about him, I said, but I had a strong sense that God wanted me in Ethan's life. So I put in a call to Bette Matkowski, the president of Johnson & Wales University, to learn more about Ethan. Bette gave me a glowing recommendation; she was impressed with his dedication to his studies and his determination to make something of his life. Soon after that, I decided to get to know Ethan better. I took him to a Colorado Rockies baseball game and invited him to my house for dinner. He later introduced me to his family and took me for an emotional visit to the scene of his accident in Fort Collins.

Over time, we formed a bond. Ethan shared his heart with me on many subjects and I shared my heart with him.

I don't condone the actions of the younger Ethan, and I still believe such acts should carry heavy legal consequences. But I also recognize the importance of personal forgiveness and redemption. Our lives are too precious to give up on them, even when we've made a tragic mistake.

I've spent a lot of time with Ethan since that lunch, helping him form a nonprofit that serves as an umbrella organization for his school presentations. Jill and I held a fund-raiser in our home for his organization, called Life CONsequences (www.lifecon.org), and I serve as its chairman of the board. Our mission is to teach young people about the dangers of social drinking, substance abuse, and the redeeming power of second chances. Not only have I become a mentor to Ethan, but I love him like the younger brother I never had. He is like family to us. I want to do everything in my power to help him succeed in transforming his life, and to prevent other young people from making the same mistakes that he made.

My connection to Ethan took an interesting twist one afternoon when I delivered a speech to The Group, Inc., a residential real estate firm based in Fort Collins. For the first time, I mentioned Ethan's story in my talk, because the accident took place in Fort Collins. After the speech, a man named Jon Holsten came over and introduced himself. He was a real estate agent and a retired police officer.

"I remember that accident," he said. "I was an officer on duty at the station that night."

He told me it was a horrific crash. But if Ethan was interested in seeing photos of the accident scene as part of his healing process, he could perhaps get access to the documents. I mentioned it to Ethan, who decided that he did want to see the photos. Jon eventually mailed me a CD with photos, which I turned over to Ethan. The pictures depicted a gruesome crash. When Ethan saw them, he broke down in convulsions, unable to stop crying for hours.

Even now he is haunted by those photos. But it's part of what keeps Ethan going, and keeps him motivated to make his nonprofit a success, to teach young people about the dangers of drinking and driving. He doesn't want anyone else to endure the pain he caused. We later received permission to use one of the photos of his totaled car in a slide show that Ethan gives; the visual evidence of the accident has a powerful impact on the student audiences who hear his talks.

Since providing us with the photos, Jon has stayed in touch; he even drove to Denver for Life CONsequence's first fund-raiser. Ethan later spoke at a monthly meeting of The Group, Inc., and we honored Jon for the role he played in Ethan's healing. At the end of that presentation, the real estate agents in attendance passed the hat and raised $4,200 for Ethan's charity.

I'm convinced that Ethan is on his way to making an important contribution to society. He has already changed hundreds of lives among the countless youth he has talked to across the country. He's changed my life as well. I realize how much I've grown since meeting him. I recognize now that not everyone who is sent to prison is a lost cause or a lost soul. My relationship with Ethan, as well as the prison experiences I had at Darrington and Angola, have helped me understand that an individual convicted of a crime can be a good person who made a terrible choice and who deserves a second chance in life.

Ethan made some bad choices; he would never argue about that. But what impresses me about Ethan is that he is working so hard to make amends. "Prison was easy compared to what I face every day," he acknowledges. "I wake up every morning knowing that I killed an innocent man."

Ethan could have given up when he was unable to find a job or an apartment—he could have gone back to the mind-numbing narcotics of drugs and alcohol. Instead, he's trying to make a positive difference in the world. By doing everything he can to make a wrong a right, Ethan is proof that changing your heart—and acting on that belief—is a crucial step toward heart-led leadership.

Second Daughter: Nikki's Story

FIVE YEARS AGO MY WIFE AND I DECIDED TO HIRE A NANNY TO HELP with child care. Since I was on the road frequently and couldn't always be there to help Jill with the daily tasks involved in raising three children and managing a house, we thought hiring a nanny was the right solution.

After getting some recommendations from friends and interviewing several candidates, we decided to hire an impressive young woman from Virginia, an honors graduate of the College of William & Mary who was looking for a temporary job before leaving to join the Peace Corps. She was someone we knew we could trust, and we thought she would be an excellent role model for our children.

Just before we completed the details, though, my wife suggested that we interview one more candidate, a young woman named Nikki who was related to a family friend in Santa Fe, New Mexico. Nikki had led a tough life, and her mother, Teresa, thought it would benefit her daughter to leave Santa Fe for a period of time. She asked us to consider Nikki for our nanny position.

"I'm sorry, Jill," I said half jokingly, "but the application process is closed."

"Well then, I guess you are going to have to reopen the application process," she retorted. "It's not going to hurt you to have a conversation."

Although I thought we'd selected the right applicant, I relented and agreed to speak with Nikki's mother. Teresa told me Nikki was a good kid who had never done drugs and who had a strong work ethic. "But she's had a very tough life. She needs a change. She will work very hard for your family," she said.

Teresa offered to email us a picture of Nikki. The photo we received was of a young Hispanic woman with a warm smile wearing a white tank top. But as I focused more clearly on the picture, I noticed multiple piercings in Nikki's ears and colorful tattoos across her chest, arms, and neck. I could barely see her skin beneath all the tattoos. And for some reason I just couldn't get past the tattoos. I showed the photo to Jill and said, "There is no way we are hiring a nanny with all these tattoos to come live with us and help raise our children."

Jill counseled me to keep an open mind. "Everyone has a story," she said. "Nikki may not be right for us, but at least take the time to talk with her."

So I reluctantly set up a phone conversation with Nikki. I figured I'd talk to her for 10 minutes, be done with it, and then go forward with our original plan.

When we finally talked on the phone, I began by asking Nikki to tell me about a bit about herself. And what I heard over the next few minutes completely floored me. Nikki's story was not pretty and she didn't spare any details. Her father was addicted to drugs and alcohol and was frequently in prisons or hospitals. Worse was the sexual abuse that she suffered from various men, starting as early as middle school. Nikki dropped out of school at age 16 to help raise her nephews after her mother had obtained custody of them from Nikki's sister. She told me the story of her first marriage, when she was 20 years old, and of the emotional and physical abuse she had suffered at the hands of a husband who was later sent to prison. What was supposed to be a 10 minute conversation turned into more than an hour.

I listened to all of this in a state of shock. As a father of young children, I was sick at the thought of the terrible things that had happened to Nikki. I didn't know what to say in response. I also had a hard time envisioning hiring a woman with this troubled background to care for my children. But there seemed to be something special about Nikki. I could hear the goodness in her voice. I could tell that the abuse she'd endured hadn't hardened her heart. She was truly fighting to be loved. And I sensed that she had much untapped love to give to others. I could also tell that she was a nurturing person when she described her past jobs, which included taking care of a disabled elderly man and working at the Boys and Girls Club, where she once saved the life of a young autistic boy who nearly drowned in the pool.

Later, after talking through my mixed feelings with Jill, I called some of my best friends and mentors in Denver, Jerry Middel and Scott Bemis. They both told me the same thing; I had to think of my family, but it was also important to consider how I could change this young woman's life by giving her a chance. "If you bring her into your house," Jerry said to me, "you can model for her what it means to love and to be loved."

Still conflicted, I placed a phone call to the young woman in Virginia to whom we had been planning to offer the job. I told her about Nikki, not even knowing where I wanted our conversation to go.

"Mr. Spaulding," she said when I was finished, "you have to hire Nikki. God is trying to tell you something. The truth is, I'm looking for a job for a year, but Nikki is looking for a family."

In the end, we took that advice and hired Nikki. When Jill and I called and offered her the job as our nanny, she accepted on the spot. She was so excited to have a new start in life that she didn't even ask us about her salary.

When Nikki came to live with us soon after that, two things were readily apparent. One, Nikki was an incredible worker. She helped with child care, she cooked, she cleaned, and she even dealt with the electricians and plumbers who came to our house. No task fazed her, and she had an enviable work ethic. At the same time, though, she had a bit of a chip on her shoulder as a result of the problems she had faced growing up. She was unsure of herself in her personal relationships and had a major issue with trust, especially when it came to men. For instance, I'm a big hugger, but the first time I tried to hug Nikki, she turned sideways and backed away from me.

But over time Nikki slowly opened up. We could see her progress over the months as she made more eye contact. As she became comfortable with our family and more confident in herself, she was able to accept praise, allow people to touch her, and show affection more easily. She went from being a wary, defensive person who always had her guard up to a young woman who was able to express herself with warmth and love.

"When I first moved to Colorado," Nikki said, "I was kind of afraid that I was going to work for a rich white family that was going to judge me. And I didn't have the foundation growing up that would let me appreciate how a family could love each other and love me. But when I started to see how much love there was in the family, and when Tommy and Jill kept telling me how much they appreciated me and how much they loved me, it helped me learn how to receive love."

Over time, a softer side to Nikki emerged. She discovered that she was skilled at being a caretaker and a nurturer; she cared for our children as though they were her own. And our three kids grew to love her. I have fond memories, for instance, of my son Tate frequently curled up in Nikki's arms. Nikki became such a loved and valued part of our family that Jill began affectionately calling her "our tattooed angel."

Nikki ended up living with us for three years. During

that time, she reconnected with a boyfriend from high school on one of her trips home to Santa Fe. When their friendship developed into more of a relationship, I told Nikki that I wanted to meet him. So he made a trip to Denver to spend time with our family.

Let me tell you, Nikki's boyfriend, Marcial, is a tattooed giant of a man—6'4" and 270 pounds—but he is an absolute teddy bear with a huge heart. When Marcial met me for the first time, he gave me a bear hug that practically lifted me off the ground. And he told me, "You were the first man who ever showed real love to Nikki. Thank you." I knew right away that he was a good man who would treat Nikki well.

Nikki eventually returned to New Mexico to be with Marcial and start a new life with him. It was a bittersweet moment for our family, because we were proud and sad at the same time. But although Nikki and Marcial live in a different city now, they will forever be a part of our family. Nikki has made several trips back to Denver to visit us and to see our children on birthdays or other special occasions. And when she comes back, it's as if she never left—our kids run up and hug her and shower her with love. During one visit, she came walking into the house waving a piece of paper with a huge smile on her face—she was holding her newly earned high school diploma.

Nikki's time with our family changed us all. And Nikki found her purpose and grew to become a loving and confident young woman. It was heartwarming to watch her grow and to know that our family played a part in helping her turn around her life.

But our family got so much more out of having Nikki work for us than just a nanny. Nikki taught our family about perseverance and about overcoming obstacles. I suspect most people would have crumbled or given up in the face of the kind of childhood she endured. But Nikki exhibited the most amazing courage and strength. I also learned a lot about people who grow up abused. Before meeting Nikki, I believed that people could always choose to move or leave if they were in a bad situation. Now I know that it's not that easy to break free of such an environment.

But the most important thing I learned has to do with acceptance and love. After all, this is a woman I was opposed to hiring because I didn't like how she looked and because I was afraid of her hardscrabble upbringing. But by the time she left us, I no longer saw the tattoos on her body—I could only see Nikki and her beautiful heart. She may have learned about love, opening up, and letting go during her three years with our family, but I learned about love right alongside her. My life will never be the same, and it's all because—with some prodding from Jill—I chose to listen with my heart.

I once asked Nikki what she felt she had learned during her time with us.

"It taught me to face life head-on," she told me, "and also that I have to let people love me. I learned about what love really is, and it helped me grow into the person I'm supposed to be. When I took the job, I thought I'd work as a nanny for a while and get some experience and then probably never see your family again. I had no idea how it would change my life. You filled a void in my heart. I didn't know when I came to Colorado that, by the time I left, I would love you as my parents."

I gave her a big hug.

Before she returned to New Mexico, Nikki called the family together and said she had something important to share with us. So we all huddled in the kitchen—Nikki and Marcial, Jill, myself, and our three children, Anthony, Caroline, and Tate.

Nikki looked at me and spoke slowly.

"Tommy, you've become like a father to me. You've helped me grow as a person and you've loved me like no other man in my life has ever loved me," she said. Choked up, she continued, "I've talked about this with Marcial and with my mom, and I told them that you're one of the people I want to remember on the most important day of my life. So Tommy, I'd be honored, when Marcial and I marry, if you would walk me down the aisle."

Right there in front of my wife and children, I broke down and cried.

I gave Nikki a hug and said, "Yes, yes, of course I will walk you down the aisle on your wedding day. It would be my honor."

Marcial was smiling. My children were excited. Jill's

eyes were moist and she had a proud look on her face. We had come so far with our tattooed angel.

Nikki is forever going to be part of the *heart*print I leave on this world; my family and I are blessed to have this amazing young woman in our lives. And it's all because we set aside preconceived notions and fears and made a commitment to accept and to love and to live with our hearts.

That young woman from Virginia was right. Nikki wasn't looking for a job; she was looking for a family. And while I may have been looking for a nanny, in the end I gained a second daughter.

Conclusion: Win for Tomorrow

T ERRY, ETHAN, AND NIKKI ALL OFFER LESSONS IN THE POWER OF
second chances. But there's something even more uni-
versal at play in their stories—and in all the stories I've
shared. The *heart*prints left by the individuals all tie back
to the 18-inch journey of heart-led leadership—the leadership philosophy I've tried to point out in this book.

Terry Adams, my first boss out of college, offered me a
second chance years ago when I found myself dumbstruck
on that auditorium stage while trying to give an introduction to an Up with People show. That *heart*print in my journey helped me learn to believe in myself, to never give up,
and to breathe that type of encouragement into the lives
of others.

Ethan Fisher, the could-have-been basketball star who
fell to addiction, hit rock bottom when he was sentenced
to prison but then found redemption and a chance to
turn his life around through education, hard work, and

self-forgiveness. Burl Cain and Grove Norwood helped me rethink long-held views about crime, punishment, and forgiveness. It has made me a more empathetic person.

And Nikki, the young woman who spent three years helping care for my children, demonstrated courage and determination in overcoming abusive relationships and then learned to accept the love of others and to share her own love. That *heart*print in my journey reminded me of the importance of modeling love toward others when it isn't the easy or obvious choice.

These *heart*prints weren't just second chances along my journey; they were *next* chances. Chances, as Tee Green puts it, to "win for tomorrow."

"You have to plant the seeds for the future," Tee said to me. "I believe that if we can create a culture where our people choose to impact others positively, then we will win for tomorrow.

"I always tell my teams, 'Leadership doesn't have anything to do with one's title. Every one of you is a leader if you impact people.' If we don't impact people positively, then we may win short-term but not long-term. I would argue that the organization that focuses on these things—on serving others, on impacting others positively, and on leading with your heart—is the organization that will always win for tomorrow."

TO ME, THE COMPANY that focuses on serving others, on impacting others positively, and on leading with the heart will win for tomorrow in two ways. It will enjoy increased sales, higher profits, greater employee engagement, reduced turnover, stronger teams, more efficient operations, and more consistent innovation. It will also change people's lives for the better.

So whether you're leading an organization or are an individual looking to create change in your own life, or that of your family, or your community, heart-led leadership isn't about a title.

It's about serving others. It's about having an impact. It's about love.

I believe heart-led leadership sets you up to turn every next chance into a win for tomorrow—for yourself and, more important, for everyone around you.

My experiences with the Who Leaders you've met in this book have, over the course of many years, sparked a revolution in me that has inspired me to live and lead differently. It has made me want to become a better human being. It has taught me the greatest of all leadership lessons: that who we are is a reflection of how we love, lead, and serve others.

Arsène Houssaye, a 19th-century French novelist and poet, once said, "Tell me whom you love and I will tell you who you are." I couldn't agree more. The person you are today is largely the result of the people you've met, befriended, interacted with, and loved in your life—not just spouses and family members, but neighbors, friends, co-workers, clients, and colleagues.

People often ask me for insights into growing their organizations. The formula isn't complicated, I tell them. If you want to grow your organization, first you have to grow your relationships. And if you want to grow your relationships, first you have to grow your heart. And if you want to grow your heart—if you want to be a heart-led Who Leader—first you need to act from a place of love in everything you do and with everyone you meet.

This doesn't mean you have to hug people at work, tell them you love them, make emotional speeches, or use happy-face emoticons in your emails. Heart-led leadership is a philosophy. You saw what that philosophy looks like in the pages of this book. It's about approaching life with a passion for loving and serving others, in order to win for tomorrow.

If you want to change your business, your life, your world, then I encourage you to embark on the 18-inch journey of heart-led leadership. I am certain that you will find your own unique way to love, lead, and serve others.

Walt Rakowich and Cheryl Bachelder turned around failing businesses. Frank DeAngelis turned around the culture of a school marred by tragedy. Burl Cain turned around a violent prison. Those achievements, however, don't represent who they are. Those achievements happened *because* of who they are. That is what truly matters.

As I said at the outset of this book, love and results are two sides of the same coin. As a leader, you never have to choose between love and results—rather, strive for love-*driven* results.

If you approach every next chance listening to who you

are and leading with your heart, I believe you will have a profound impact on the lives of the people you touch and the organizations you lead. Everything comes down to your heart. Whatever the question, love is the answer. The truth is, you can't truly lead people without loving them, too. And people will always know the difference.

Because love wins.

ACKNOWLEDGMENTS

TO MY GHOSTWRITER AND LIFELONG FRIEND BOB RIEL, FOR NOT TREAT-ing this book like a job, but as a chance to bring heart-led leadership to the world.

To my literary consultant and dear friend Michael Palgon, for taking a chance on me with my first book and mentoring me through this second book.

To my editor, Roger Scholl, and the entire Penguin Random House team—thank you for pushing me to find the real "heart" on these pages.

To Rick Barrera and Stephen Caldwell, for your friendship and for helping take *The Heart-Led Leader* to the next level.

To my longtime director of business development, Debbie LeBleu, for not only believing in my message, but for living it every day.

To my executive assistant and business manager, Lindsey Blomberg, for all the things you do behind the scenes that help our team change the world.

To our ROR (Return on Relationships), BUILD BIKES BENEFIT, and the 18-INCH JOURNEY (to Heart-Led Leadership) trainer, Duane Grischow, for treating all of our clients like they were your very first.

To the entire Brooks & Spaulding speaking management team and my partner, Maureen Brooks, for your commitment to bringing heart-led leadership to organizations across the globe.

To my true friend and executive director of the Spaulding Leadership Institute, Cathy DeGraff, for all the hundreds and thousands of lives you touch, especially mine.

To Jen Moody and all the donors and volunteers of the Ben Graebel National Leadership Academy—thank you for helping change the hearts and minds of thousands of young heart-led leaders.

To the Heart of Leaders participants at the Center for Heart-Led Leadership, for believing in our vision and, more important, for not being afraid to take the 18-inch journey.

To the St. Louis "Fab-Eight": Jim Wipke, Jill Scheulen, Dustin Odham, Matt Miller, Terry Harris, Nisha Patel, Cindy Carey, and Jennifer Strauser, for your commitment to changing public education.

To Joe Krenn and Farmington Country Club in Charlottesville, Virginia, for your friendship and generosity in hosting our quarterly 5th Floor Men's Retreats.

To Brad Billingsley, one of the best executive coaches I know—for your heart and our special friendship.

To Ken Blanchard, Phyllis Hendry, Jimmy Blanchard, and my Lead Like Jesus family, for always reminding me who the greatest leadership role model ever was.

To my mentors Jerry Middel, Scott Bemis, and Scott Lynn, for the *heart*print you have made on my life. Thank you for pushing me to become a better husband, father, and human being.

To my friend and the most talented writer that I know, Eric Blehm, for teaching me to live *Fearless*.

To Corey Turer, my best friend since we were kids.

To all the heart-led leaders who have inspired me to write this book: I hope, through your example, others will follow and realize that love and results are two sides of the same coin.

To my parents, Tom and Angie Spaulding and Diane and Lou Marino, for your unconditional love and belief in me.

To my sisters, Lisa Kevins and Michele Kelly, for carrying on Popa's legacy of "family, family, and family!"

To Nikki, Marcial, and Ethan Fisher, for teaching me what the 18-inch journey is all about.

To our children: Anthony, Caroline, and Tate—your mother and I could not be more proud of the young men and woman you are growing to become. We love you to the moon and back. Always remember our family motto, GFO: *God, Family,* and serving *Others.*

To my wife, Jill, who is a much better human being than I. Being married to you is a God-given gift, a blessing, and an honor.

And to my heavenly Father—"And we know that in all things God works for the good of those who love Him." (Romans 8:28)

INDEX

Darrington Unit, Houston, 46–48, 215
DeAngelis, Frank, 5, 61–67, 230
Death-to-summit ratio, 89, 96
Decision making, bottom-line, 57
Delaney, Brian, 121–123
Dickson, Lisa, 138
Dignity, 77, 80, 82, 185
DiLoreto, Steve, 142
Discretionary efforts, 4
Disney Corporation, 155
Dixon, Rod, 69–72
Drug use, 104, 106
Drunk driving, 206–215

Earth Treks, 94–95
Effort, 88
18-inch journey, 1, 3, 7, 36, 46, 193
    authenticity, 57, 97–102, 129
    caring, 76–82
    character, 117–123
    empathy, 2, 57, 153–157
    encouragement, 147–151
    faithfulness, 111–116
    forgiveness, 42–45, 49, 51, 136–139, 228
    generosity, 2, 57, 155, 156, 161–166
    honesty, 98, 167–172, 184, 185, 187
    humility, 57, 71–73, 98, 184, 187
    love, 2, 4, 55–58, 61–67, 193, 194, 221–225, 229–231
    passion, 85–88
    purpose, 141–145
    self-awareness, 103–107
    selflessness, 57, 90–96
    transparency, 57, 133, 167, 170, 181–188
    trust, 173–180, 184–185
    vulnerability, 57, 128–133, 184–187
Empathy, 2, 57, 153–157
Encouragement, 147–151
Enthusiasm, 88

Extreme Leadership Committee, 56, 103

Faithfulness, 111–116
False modesty, 73
Farber, Steve, 56
Fast-food industry, 76–80
Fearless (Blehm), 201
Fillmore, Millard, 159–160
Fisher, Ethan, 194, 205–215, 227–228
Forgiveness, 42–45, 49, 51, 136–139, 228
Franchise business, 77–79
Frank, 135–137
French, Jay Jay, 103–107

Garfield, James, 160
Generosity, 2, 57, 155, 156, 161–166
Gilmore, Rusty, 43, 47
Graebel, Bill, 97–101
Graebel Companies, 97–100
Green, Ted, 5, 27, 37
Green, Tee, 15–25, 228
Greenway Health, 5, 15–25, 27
Group Inc., The, 213
Grunden, Eric, 18–20

Hairston, Mike, 18–19
Hamby, Jay, 85–87
Harris, Eric, 62
Harrison, Benjamin, 159–160
Harrison, William Henry, 160
Hayes, John, 141–145
Heart-led leadership philosophy, 2–7, 228–231
    Adams, Terry and, 194, 196–203, 227
    Bachelder, Cheryl and, 5, 75–82, 230
    Cain, Burl and, 6, 44–46, 49, 50, 228, 230
    Craig, David and, 119–121
    DeAngelis, Frank and, 5, 61–67, 230
    Delaney, Brian and, 121–123

ABOUT THE AUTHOR

TOMMY SPAULDING is the founder and president of Spaulding Companies, a leadership development, speaking, training, consulting, and executive coaching firm based in Denver, Colorado. A world-renowned speaker on leadership, Spaulding has addressed hundreds of organizations, associations, educational institutions, and corporations around the globe. His first book, *It's Not Just Who You Know: Transform Your Life (and Your Organization) by Turning Colleagues and Contacts into Lasting, Genuine Relationships*, published by Penguin Random House in 2010, quickly climbed to the top of the *New York Times, Wall Street Journal,* and *USA Today* national bestseller lists.

Spaulding rose to become the youngest president and CEO of the world-renowned leadership organization Up with People. In 2000, he founded Leader's Challenge, which grew to become the largest high school civic and leadership program in the state of Colorado. He is the founder and president of the Global Youth Leadership Academy as well as the National Leadership Academy, a leading national nonprofit high school leadership development organization.

Tommy Spaulding is also the cofounder and president of The Center for Heart-Led Leadership, a speaking management firm and executive leadership development organization that runs the Heart of Leaders programs.

Spaulding received a BA in Political Science from East Carolina University (1992); an MBA from Bond University in Australia (1998), where he was a Rotary Ambassadorial Scholar; and an MA in Non-Profit Management from Regis University (2005).

In 2006, Spaulding was awarded the Outstanding Alumni Award by East Carolina University (ECU), and in 2007, he received an honorary PhD in humanities from the Art Institute of Colorado. In 2009, he was appointed ECU's first "Leader in Residence."

In September 2012, Spaulding was named by *Meetings and Conventions* magazine as one of the 100 Most Favorite Speakers in the nation.

Tommy Spaulding resides in the Denver metropolitan area with his wife and children.

SUCCESS IS NOT DETERMINED BY WHO YOU KNOW, BUT BY HOW WELL THEY KNOW YOU

"In *It's Not Just Who You Know,* Tommy Spaulding delivers his ideas and life experiences in a way that can really help people achieve relationship excellence. This book should be required reading."

—Lee Cockerell, executive vice president (retired)
of Walt Disney World Resort

TRANSFORM YOUR LIFE (AND YOUR ORGANIZATION)
BY TURNING COLLEAGUES AND CONTACTS
INTO LASTING, GENUINE RELATIONSHIPS

It's Not
Just
Who
You
Know

TOMMY SPAULDING
FOREWORD BY KEN BLANCHARD

Tommy Spaulding, *New York Times* bestselling author, overcame enormous obstacles on his path to success, beginning with the dyslexia that hamstrung his academic career. What shaped and powered his extraordinary achievements in every area of his life were his relationships with people. In this compelling, story-driven narrative, Tommy reveals the nuts and bolts behind turning casual contacts and chance encounters into opportunities to create lifelong relationships.

THE CENTER
FOR
HEART LED
LEADERSHIP

SHARE THE MESSAGE

The 18-Inch Journey (to Heart-Led Leadership)

TRAINING BASED ON THE BESTSELLING BOOK

The Heart-Led Leader

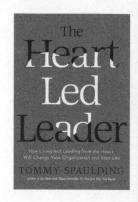

Return on Relationship (ROR)

**TRAINING BASED ON THE *NEW YORK TIMES*
BESTSELLING BOOK**

It's Not Just Who You Know

BIKE BUILD BENEFIT

*A half-day, hands on, intensive training and team-building experience
suitable for 30–300 participants*

TO LEARN MORE ABOUT SPAULDING COMPANIES' CORPORATE TRAINING PROGRAMS, VISIT

TOMMYSPAULDING.COM

SHAPING TOMORROW'S LEADERS

NATIONAL LEADERSHIP ACADEMY

Since 2000, National Leadership Academy, a high school youth leadership program, has inspired thousands of young leaders across America to become tomorrow's servant leaders.

National Leadership Academy develops and equips young people with the skills and confidence to be heart-led leaders. Our mission is to create civic and service-minded young leaders by developing their leadership skills and heart for serving others. Our vision is to spark students into action in the hope they take what they learn at the summer Academy back to their schools and communities.

In our intensive four-day summer Academy held at a private university in Denver, CO, students are mentored and taught by world-class leaders, engage in local community service projects, are challenged with outdoor team-building exercises, and develop lifelong relationships with students from across the country.

>> National Leadership Academy is a 501(c)(3) non-profit program of the Spaulding Leadership Institute.

>> To nominate a high school student or to enroll, please visit our website: www.nationalleadershipacademy.org.

This book is due on the last date stamped below.
Failure to return books on the date due may
result in assessment of overdue fees.

FINES .50 per day